RONNIE DELANY

STAYING THE DISTANCE

For my loving wife Joan;
For our wonderful children, Lisa, Ronnie,
Jennifer & Michelle, and their partners;
And for our much-loved grandchildren.

RONNIE DELANY

STAYING THE DISTANCE

THE O'BRIEN PRESS
DUBLIN

First published 2006 by The O'Brien Press Ltd,
12 Terenure Road East, Rathgar, Dublin 6, Ireland.
Tel: +353 1 4923333;
Fax: +353 1 4922777
E-mail: books@obrien.ie
Website: www.obrien.ie

ISBN-10: 0-86278-975-3
ISBN-13: 978-0-86278-975-6

British Library Cataloguing in Publication Data
Delany, Ronnie
Ronnie Delany : staying the distance
1. Delany, Ronnie 2. Runners (Sports) - Ireland - Biography
I. Title
796.4'23'092

1 2 3 4 5 6 7 8 9 10
06 07 08 09 10 11 12

Printing: MPG Books, Ltd.

PICTURES:
Cover photo, and p 83, copyright © The Melbourne Age; reproduced with permission.
Photo, front flap, from the front cover of Sports Illustrated February 2, 1959 by Richard
Meek, copyright © Sports Illustrated; used with permission.
Photographs copyright © Fred Lyon, pp 2-3, 8, 59, 66-67, 127, 144, 155, 175, 176, 177 &
180; used by kind permission of Fred Lyon.
Villanova sports photographs pp 32 (Coach Elliott), 37 (Delany & Breckenridge), 43
(Delany & IC4A Trophy), 46 (Delany & Jenkins), 146 (track team) & 154 (team), 157,
158 & 160 used by kind permission of Villanova Sports Marketing Association.
Photographs copyright © Brian Seed, pp 34, 35, 89, 90-91, 92, 96 (bottom), 97, 99, 109,
178, 187, 188; used with permission.
Photograph, p 36 © Frank Fennell Photography: used with permission.
Irish Press photograph, p 56,
Photograph, p 65, from 'The News' NYCs Picture Paper.
Independent Newspapers photographs, back flap & pp 68, 96 (top), 98, 103, 117, 123,
135; used with permission.
Irish News Agency photographs, pp 95 & 107
Philadelphia Enquirer Magazine, p 145
Photograph p 163 © Pat Maxwell Sports Photography; used with permission.
Photograph p 168 © Michael A. Purcell.
Portrait of Ronnie Delany by James Hanley, RHA, p 188, used by kind permission of
the artist.
Medals, trophies, letters, telegrams and memorabilia photographed by Emma Byrne.

TEXT:
Extracts from 'The Villanova Irish' by P.J. Browne used with permission.

ACKNOWLEDGEMENTS

I'd like to thank some of the people who inspired, helped and encouraged me to make this book a reality. Warmest thanks to:

Tony O'Reilly;
Chuck Whittington;
The IOC, Lausanne, and the Irish Olympic Council;
The staff, past and present, of *Sports Illustrated* and Time Inc.;
The staff, past and present, of Independent Newspapers and the *Irish Times*;
Frank Greally, Editor, the *Irish Runner*
Brian Seed and Fred Lyon, photographers;
Villanova University;
University of Pennsylvania:
Peter Byrne;
Des Murphy;
Leon Wiegard;
Tony O'Donoghue;
P.J. Browne;
My daughter Mimi for all her hard work on my manuscript;
My publishers, The O'Brien Press, especially Michael O'Brien, Publisher, Helen Carr, editor and Emma Byrne, designer.

Supported by BUPA Ireland.

BUPA
Ireland

Everyone at BUPA Ireland is delighted to be associated with such an important book that will for many people, young and old, evoke memories of a different era. An era when the pace of life was less hectic and champions were both scarce and genuine. Ronnie's gold medal success in Melbourne, was, and still is, a defining moment in Ireland's great sporting history. Fifty years on, his achievement is no less significant, made more so by the fact that no Irish athlete has emulated his Olympic track success since.

Ronnie's dedication to excellence in his sporting career and the success he has enjoyed in his personal and professional life since retiring from the track all those years ago makes him an ageless hero for us all. Ronnie Delany is our Ambassador for Older People; we wish him continued good health and thank him for great memories with more to come.

Beir bua agus beannacht,

Martin O'Rourke
Managing Director
BUPA Ireland

CONTENTS

INTRODUCTION
BY TONY O'REILLY

Despite the achievements of Dr Pat O'Callaghan and Robert Tisdall in more amateur times, the concept of Irish athletics was, in a sense, somewhat of a paradox. It rarely appeared on the world scene, and then only fleetingly. The 1948 Olympics in London with Jimmy Reardon, Paul Dolan and Dave Guiney gave us all a taste for world achievement, but little was forthcoming. That was, until the astounding Melbourne Olympics of 1956, probably the first truly post-World War Olympiad despite London in 1948 and Helsinki in 1952.

The 1956 Olympics coincided with my own football career and a heightened sense of the world as a stage for Irish athletes. Of all the athletes that symbolised the efforts of so many to play on a larger stage, none did so more than the hero of this book, Ronnie Delany.

Delany was a direct contemporary of mine in the early fifties at the Catholic University School, which, though fine at tennis, had never boasted a rugby team of note or an athlete who had national standing.

All this was to change with Delany, and in a period of four years, he went from 'unknown' to the greatest star the sport had ever seen in Ireland and, perhaps, in achievement, Ireland's greatest-ever sports star.

In America, his legend is unquenchable. He is the 'Villanova Rocket' – the winner of countless Wanamaker Miles at Madison Square Garden. New York took him as one of their own, and he was almost more famous there than in his native Ireland. His half mile duels with the United Kingdom's Derek Johnson in College Park in the summer of 1955 enthralled Irish athletics fans. In subsequent years at Lansdowne Road and the new Santry Stadium he took on Britain's Brian Hewson, Derek Ibbotsen and all comers in a series of classic mile races before capacity crowds.

Dublin's appetite for big time athletics had been whetted in the glory days of the late 1940s. In a succession of International Meetings at Lansdowne Road Clonliffe Harriers' irrepressible promoter Billy Morton brought over the great track mid-field stars of the time. Willie Slykhuis, Curtis Stone, Fred Wilt, Arthur Wint, E. McDonald Bailey, Harrison Dillard, Robert Richards and Jim Fuchs featured against the best of the Irish: Reardon, Dolan, Guiney, with John Joe Barry, Jack Gregory and Cummin Clancy on evenings of nostalgia and glamour.

Roger Bannister became the first man to break the 4-minute mile barrier in 1954. But Delany was to achieve what not even Bannister could achieve and that was an Olympic Gold.

On 29 November Ronnie qualified for the final of the 1,500 metres at the Melbourne Olympics in the magnificent stadium that stands to this day.

Australia's star was the great, and in their minds unbeatable, John Landy, the forerunner of extraordinary runners from the Antipodes, such as Herb Elliott, Peter Snell, John Walker, Murray Halberg and a host of other incredible middle-distance runners. It is fair to say that the 100 metres and the 1,500 metres are the two great glamour races of an Olympic meeting, and it is equally fair to say that to many field and track is 'the Olympics'. All else is exciting, interesting and unifying in a world sense, be it decathlon, pentathlon, equitation, swimming or boxing, but the Olympic ideal still surrounds track and field, and the high altar of track and field is the 100 and 1,500 metres.

With this background, the lone Irishman entered the enormous stadium as a fancied, but not favoured, runner for the final. The

Sir Anthony O'Reilly

rest is history. Delany made his break in the last bend, passed Landy, was chased by the German, Klaus Richtzenhain, and won convincingly in a time of 3 minutes 41.2 seconds, and that was an Olympic Gold.

Apart from our friendship, our fathers were also friends and worked in the Customs Service, which gave both men a great sense of purpose and pride. I rose early on the 1st of December 1956, the morning of the final, to listen to the radio broadcast (there being no television in those days) of his historic run, and when Ronnie Delany breasted the tape, I rushed into my father and shouted, 'Dad, Ronnie Delany has won the 1,500 metres for Ireland at the Melbourne Olympic Games!' My father was thoughtful for a moment, seeking a reason for this extraordinary feat, and then always the civil servant, he said to me gravely, 'Ah, yes. Of course, he's a son of a Customs Officer.'

I still pull Ronnie's leg about this kinship and the amazing deductions that people can make from certain events.

Ireland in 1956 was a poor country. Emigration was rife – almost 500,000 people emigrated in the years from 1950 to 1960. They were the years when all of us were at university, seeking jobs and looking to a new life. The sixties were to change that, and Ireland found a new sense of purpose, brought about by the First Programme of Economic Expansion, and a more outward-looking view of the world. There were many elements in this spirit of change and adventure, and one of them was Delany's win in Melbourne. It made us all feel, as a country, that we had achieved something unique, that we could compete against the best in the world, that one of us had competed at the highest level in the most singular event and triumphed.

It was a great day for Ronnie Delany and his family – it was an even greater day for Ireland.

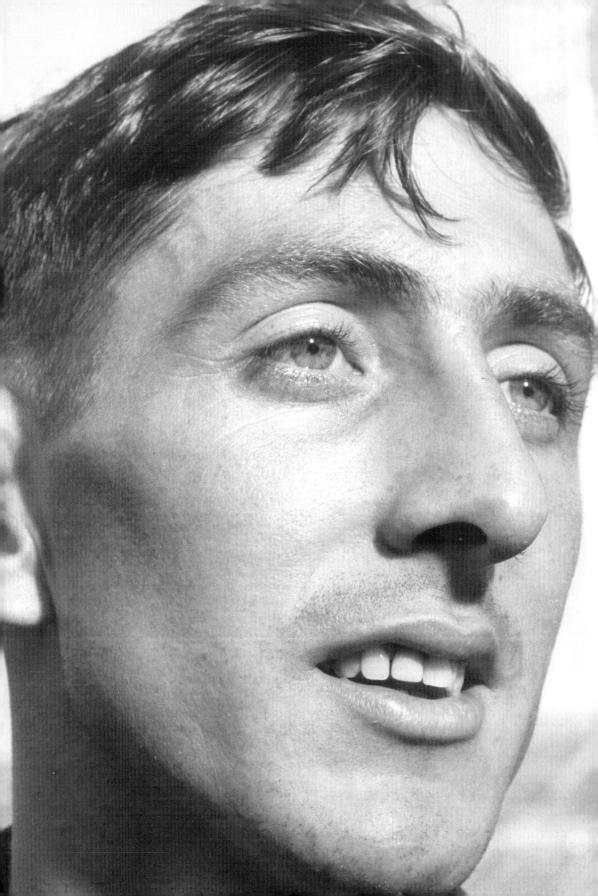

PREFACE

The breaking of the 4-minute mile barrier was a sporting event powerful enough to capture the imagination of the entire world; on 6 May 1954 a twenty-five-year-old medical student called Roger Bannister ran a mile on Oxford University's track at Iffley Road before a meagre crowd and crossed the finish line with a time of 3 minutes, 59.4 seconds. Bannister would always be remembered as the man who ran the 'miracle mile'.

For years, the 4-minute mile had been considered unreachable by the medical profession. Physiologists of the time believed it was dangerous to the health of any athlete who attempted to achieve it. The previous mile world record of 4 minutes, 01.4 seconds was set in 1945 by Gunder Haegg of Sweden. John Landy of Australia, considered one of the great milers of that era in the early fifties, had never come closer than 1:5 seconds off the 4-minute barrier before. By his achievement, Bannister may well have smashed a psychological barrier as well; within forty-six days of

Bannister's breakthrough, Landy surpassed the record with a 3-minute 57.9 seconds mile in Finland. By the end of 1957, sixteen runners had logged sub 4-minute miles.

To this day, Sir Roger Bannister's achievement remains relevant. It has inspired athletes to believe their potential is unlimited and the impossible dream is achievable. I am one he so influenced back then.

In May 1954, when Bannister was smashing the 4-minute barrier, I was a promising young Irish athlete. I had won Leinster and Irish School Championships at the half-mile or 880 yards in 1952 and 1953 in less than earth shattering times. However, in August 1953 I was to

IT ALL BEGAN WITH A SCRAPBOOK AND MAY END IN MELBOURNE

SIX years before Roger Bannister became the first man to run a mile in under four minutes, a 12-year-old boy picked up an unwanted pamphlet in his home at Sandymount, Dublin, turned it into an athletics' scrapbook, and on the cover signed his name —Ronald Delany.

Without knowing it, he had taken the first step towards joining Bannister and the other breakers of the four-minute-mile barrier eight years later.

"That was really the first time Ronnie showed of taking an interest in athletics," said Mr. P. A. Delany, a quarter and half-miler in his own image days, as he turned over the pages of his son's scrapbook last week. And I caught a glimpse of newspaper pictures of J. P. Reardon J. J. Barry and P. P. Malville Irish representatives at the London Olympic Games and heroes of the young Delany in 1948.

JOE'S EXAMPLE

"Tennis was really his first love," Mr. Delany explained, "and he smashed the youths quarter-finals at Fitzwilliam one year.

"It was the 1948 Olympic Games and, above all, the success achieved by his brother Joe in school and Leinster colleges' championships that persuaded Ronnie to leave his tennis and turn to athletics."

And, for Ronnie, a fast pace was set by Joe, who at one time, held the senior 440 yards title, the youths', intermediate and senior long jump titles.

REPEAT RIDE

Although the Irish equestrian team at the Olympics in Stockholm have not been so successful as many of us hoped they would, they have proved that, in the saddle, Irishmen and women can hold their own.

FIRST WIN

It was in 1952 that Ronnie won his first race a half-mile, at C.U.S. One year later he was beginning to match the pace set by his brother when he won the Leinster senior schools and All-Ireland schools' half-mile championships.

For business reasons, Joe has now hung up his running shoes, but Ronnie is carrying on the Delany tradition on the track against world-class opponents.

OLYMPIC HOPE?

But what are Ronnie's chances of competing in the Olympic Games in Melbourne?

"I can't help you on that question," smiled Mr. Delany, "All I know is that, because summer-time in Australia is term-time at Villanova and other American universities, students who are likely to be competing in the Games next November and December, will be given extra lectures before they leave for Melbourne."

And he handed me a cutting from an American newspaper in which the students likely to have to take extra lectures at Villanova are listed as follows: "Don Bragg, pole vaulter, Charlie Jenkins, 440 yards, and

achieve on the track in that time—well, Mr. Delany refused to play the part of a prophet. "He has plenty of stamina," represented his only comment.

"Was it a complete surprise to me when Ronnie ran his four-minute mile?" he echoed. "Not a complete surprise. I judged that the 4.4 he had done on boards, with nine laps to the mile, would represent a time of 4.1 or under on the track, with four laps to the mile."

Maybe, Mr. Delany will see his son running a mile in less than four minutes at Lon-

When Ronnie Delany reaches Dublin to-day (Tuesday), Mr. and Mrs. P. A. Delany will welcome home the first Irishman to run a mile in less than four minutes. Before he

packed his bags and boarded the plane, Ronnie added another record to his collection when he won the 1,500 metres in 3 minutes 47.3 seconds in a National Collegiate A.A. meet-

ing at Berkeley, California, last Sunday. He finished two yards ahead of Jim Bailey, the Australian runner who recently beat the mile. Eight men have now accomplished this feat.

13

become the first Irish schoolboy to break the 'two-minute barrier' when winning a men's half-mile race in College Park in a time of 1 minute, 58.7 seconds.

I didn't know it at the time, but this achievement was to change my life. I immediately began to realise that I had been gifted with a special talent for running. I knew then that I wanted to be a great athlete and no one, and no circumstance, was going to deter me. With dedication that surprised even me, I took control of my own life and made decisions with the foremost goal of furthering my athletics career. Luckily, the results came with extraordinary frequency, allowing me to build success on success.

In 1954 I had yet to run a mile and had never once been outside Ireland. Two years later I was to become only the seventh runner in the world, and the youngest ever, to break the still magical 4-minute barrier. On 1 June 1956 in a competitive mile race in Compton, California I ran a time of 3-minutes, 59 seconds. That same year, six months to the day later, I was crowned Olympic Champion at the Melbourne Olympic Games.

In a hotly contested final of the 1,500 metres I won gold for Ireland to the surprise of a partisan crowd of 120,000 Australians who were cheering on their hero and the race favourite John Landy. I was twenty-one years of age, and I felt that I had achieved my destiny. For the second time in my young life a sporting achievement was to irrevocably influence my future.

Much has been written then and since about my Olympic victory. The story is revisited at least every four years at the time of successive Olympic Games. I will be forever grateful to the Irish public who congratulate me to this day on my Olympic achievement as if it were yesterday. Somehow the mystique of being an Olympic Champion, the achievement of winning a gold medal lives on. I recall one such occasion when I was walking along the North Quays in Dublin and was confronted by a 'real Dub' who, with interspersed expletives, asked me if I was Ronnie Delany. I replied modestly that I was. He eyeballed me deliberately and said, 'You know what, I never saw anyone get so much bloody mileage out of winning a medal!'

To this day some fifty years later people still ask me where it all began. Were you very talented as a youngster? How did you recognise your great ability? Where were you born, and so forth? In short, I have been beguiled and encouraged to write my memoirs, to recall the past and satisfy the curiosity of the many who 'just want to know'. Above all, I hope my story will be interesting and bring into perspective a different era in sport. I hope I can paint a picture of what it was like for a young Irishman to leave a depressed Ireland in the fifties, a land of no opportunity, and take on the world in sport.

Opposite: A moment of prayerful thanksgiving after winning the 1,500-metre final, 1 December 1956.

EARLY YEARS

All my life I have been proud of my origins in Co. Wicklow. The *Liber Baptizatorum* entry in the register of St Joseph's Church, Templerainey just outside Arklow records that I was born on 6 March 1935 in a house called Hillview, Ferrybank, baptised on 10 March 1935, confirmed on 26 June 1945 and married to Joan Mary Riordan on 30 August 1962. My father Patrick Antonius Delany was from Batterstown, Co. Meath and my dearest mother Brigid Maria Hughes from Dublin, near Leeson Street Bridge. Dad's family were farmers in Co. Meath

and Mammy's dad, Joseph Hughes, was a publican at 8/9 Sussex Terrace, Dublin 4. The pub, which Grandad sold in 1949, is now known as O'Brien's, and is a popular watering hole for many southsiders.

Opposite Left: A studio shot of my mother, Brigid Maria Hughes, c. 1920.
This page: *Granny & Grandad Hughes and their family (l to r) Annie, John, Mollie and Joe, with Michael and Mum behind them.*

Around the time I was born my father was a customs and excise officer and we lived in Hillview for five or six years before the family moved to Dublin. The house where I was born is believed to have been part of the Wicklow estate of Lord Wicklow when built in or around the 1860s. In 2001, Arklow Chamber of Commerce erected a commemorative plaque outside with the simple inscription, 'Birthplace of Ronnie Delany, Olympic Gold Medallist 1,500 metres Melbourne 1956'. I remain deeply appreciative of this gesture for although the family moved to Dublin my mother and I, in particular, maintained close links with friends in the Arklow and Avoca areas. I have many wonderful child-

hood memories of my early years living in Hillview with the Avoca River flowing by the back of the house, which had many rooms and very steep stairs inside.

One strong memory from my childhood is my father's love of stories and anecdotes. A favourite one referred to his years as a Customs and Excise Officer in Arklow. He mistakenly requisitioned an amount of blotting paper from Head Office in Dublin. He meant to order four or five 'quires', or about a hundred sheets, but instead ordered four or five reams, or a couple of thousand sheets! To his horror, a few days later a horse-drawn cart from Arklow Railway Station drew up outside his offices in town with a massive load of unwanted blotting paper, which he quickly secreted in a spare office. What was Dad to do? At the very least it would be embarrassing to advise Head Office of his error. How he managed to off-load the blotting paper demonstrated his ingenuity and lateral thinking – for months afterwards every unsuspecting pensioner who called to his office was seen to leave with armfuls of the dreaded blotting paper. As a child, I loved this story and enjoyed hearing Dad tell it.

This misadventure did not affect his career prospects. Just after the start of the Second World War Dad was promoted and transferred to Dublin. We moved *en famille* to live at 'Melrose', 33 St John's Road, Sandymount. At this date, I had two older brothers, Joe and Paddy, and a younger and beautiful sister, Colette. Sandymount was where I grew up, in an environment that was to have an

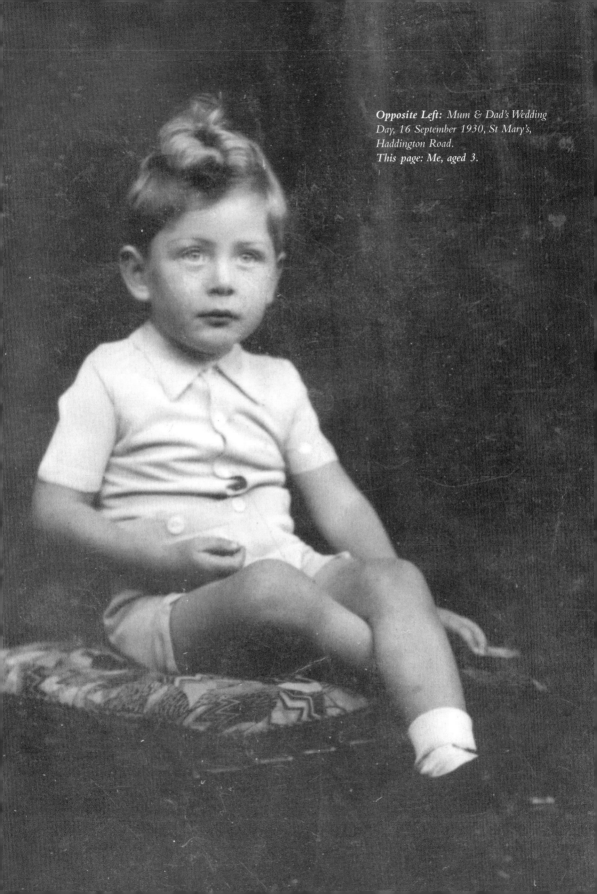

Opposite Left: Mum & Dad's Wedding Day, 16 September 1930, St Mary's, Haddington Road.
This page: Me, aged 3.

extraordinary impact on my development into a world-class athlete.

My earliest memories of St John's Road are of hot summer days and the discomfort of once being sunburnt, with Mammy applying copious amounts of Nivea cream to relieve the pain. Sandymount Strand was the nearest beach to the inner city and literally thousands of Dublin families travelled the few miles outbound for a day at the seaside. The beach often became so crowded on an incoming tide that the throngs spilled over on to the Strand Road and the nearby streets, including St John's Road. The sight of happy families pic-nicking on the pavements, light-ing fires to boil their kettles and really enjoying themselves lives on in my memory to this day.

Winter months during my earliest years were filled with the joy of the Delany family gathered together in the living room listening to the radio. In those days, radio broadcasts of heavy-weight fights from Madison Square Garden, New York were an extraordinary opportunity to bond with your Da and siblings. Getting up to listen in what seemed like the middle of the night because of the time difference, huddling around the crackling radio and visualising Joe Louis the Brown Bomber in full flight as he put away another pretender to his throne are enthralling childhood memories.

The victorious CUS team, Leinster Inter-School Lawn Tennis Competition 1953. Front row, Ronan Fearon (centre), Robert Davitt and Maurice Rafter, with (back row l-r) Ronnie Delany, Jimmy O'Connell, Eimhear MacCarvill and David Jackson.

Sandymount and its environs were to provide an unrivalled haven for a youngster madly inter-ested in sport. Behind our house on St John's Road was Claremont Lawn Tennis Club where in my teens I spent gloriously happy days play-ing my favourite sport – tennis. Behind Claremont was Railway Union Sports Club and its multiple playing fields where I learned to play hockey, cricket and lawn bowls as well as honing my skills later as a runner and sometimes rugby player. My bedroom window at the back of our house looked out on Claremont. During the long summer evenings, after I was sent up to bed, I spent hours looking out in wonder at court seven and the senior players, clad in pristine tennis whites, displaying an array of shots and skills way beyond my early competence. And if this wasn't enough, the Sandymount Strand and its shallow waters were just up the road. Remarkably, I never did learn how to swim until my late twenties. This arguably was a good thing for swimming developed muscles not conducive to running, according to expert opinion at the time.

I was too young when living in Arklow to show any appreciative talent in sport and no one has ever volunteered any information to the contrary. Apparently I was not a budding young athletic star as, say, Tiger Woods was in his childhood. However, living in Sandymount was to prove different. Once I could lift a racquet or swing a bat the spontaneous thing to do was to go out and play sport. This I did with abandon during every free moment in my formative years. In the process I was progressively developing my athleticism and, unknowingly, my overall body strength.

My earliest memory of showing any promise as a runner was when I was twelve. I, along with Niall Brophy, Derrick Gygax and Paul Cauldwell, was selected for a relay team to compete in the primary school sports team representing my school, O'Connells CBS in North Richmond Street. O'Connells almost backed onto Croke Park and the sports were held in this great stadium. I am indebted to Paul Cauldwell who told me recently that I ran lead-

off handing over to him for the second leg. Derrick took the baton from Paul and passed it on to the flying Brophy for the last leg. We won of course or I would not be telling the story! To this day, Niall Brophy – who subsequently gained twenty-one caps on the Irish Rugby team in the late fifties and early sixties and went on two British and Irish Lions Tours – unkindly claims that I was the slowest runner on the team. Derrick Gygax emigrated to Canada and represented his adopted country in the Olympic marathon. Paul Cauldwell successfully played senior level soccer for Fairview CYMS for many years. Not too bad a quartet by any standards.

The O'Connells School annual sports and drill displays were also held in Croke Park. I can recall one such sports day when I had the distinction of winning the wheelbarrow race. I was the barrow and pushing me to victory was a classmate, Chris Baxter. The prize was a two-pound pot of Kavanagh's Raspberry jam, which I received as proudly as if it were an Olympic gold medal. But I was to be undone; my eldest brother Joe, who was the outstanding schoolboy athlete of his era in Ireland, won four or five events and the equivalent number of pots of jam. Why Kavanagh's were sponsoring the jammy prizes I do not know!

I like recalling the relay win and the wheelbarrow race in Croke Park for it was an incredible experience for a youngster to run and play sport on the hallowed turf of this great stadium steeped in the history and folklore of our national games of hurling and football. During the 1980s I was frequently a guest of the Gaelic Athletic Association in Croke Park in my capacity as Chairman of Cospóir, the National Sports

Council. I always felt I had an insider's knowledge of the lush green playing pitch. But I confess I was slow to share it with the distinguished personages who filled the Ard Comhairle on those great Sunday afternoons in September each year.

O'Connells CBS holds a special place in the history of Ireland in the early part of the last century. Called after Daniel O'Connell, the school has produced a distinguished number of scholars, politicians and sportsmen. From the literary world Oliver St John Gogarty and Thomas Kinsella, to name but two; two Presidents Sean T. O'Ceallaigh and Cearbhall Ó Dálaigh, and Taoiseachs John A. Costello and Sean Lemass; from the sporting milieu, such luminaries as Michael O'Hehir, Sean Óg O'Ceallaghain, Robbie Kelleher, Eoin Hand, and the legendary golfer Joe Carr, winner of three British Amateur Championships. Pat

Kenny and Jim Sherwin also went to O'Connell's.

There is one dimension of my attendance at O'Connell's Primary School that I believe has a particular relevance to my development into a world-class athlete. I travelled daily to and from school on the train from Sydney Parade station to Amiens Street station, and also made a rushed journey home and back at lunchtime. I ran to Sydney Parade in the morning and from Amiens Street, up the steep incline of Buckingham Street, to be on time for school. At lunchtime I raced my brother Joe home from Sydney Parade to St John's Road in a futile effort to be first home. The prize was the scrapings of the pot, the residue of Mammy's lovely rice or semolina milk pudding.

Unknowingly, I was 'clocking up the mileage', in running parlance, developing my leg strength and cardiovascular system. Much has been written about the latter-day emergence of the great Kenyan and other African runners who live at altitude and run miles and miles to and from school. It is seriously argued that this fact is very significant in their ability to set world distance running records and win Olympic titles. The contrast is made with the sedentary lifestyle of the Americans who seldom, if ever, produce a distance runner.

There was nothing noteworthy about my sporting success or otherwise in my early teens. I left O'Connells and went for a while to the local Sandymount High School set up by a former O'Connells teacher Patrick Cannon. Sandymount High had a very limited sports programme with the curriculum of the school focused on academic accomplishment. I played my sports in Claremont and Railway Union, and because my brother Joe was winning all round him in Leinster and Irish School and Youths Championships, especially in the long jump where he excelled, I naturally joined the local athletics club, Crusaders AC.

Crusaders trained at Churchill Terrace in Sandymount and I came under the influence of my first coach, Brendan Hennessy – a delightful

Opposite Left: Confirmation Day, 1945. Ronnie Delany, 2nd row from back, 5th in from the right. Chris Baxter, the 'pusher' in the wheelbarrow race, is 2nd row, 3rd from right.
This page: *B.J. Fitzpatrick, O'Connell's Schools PPU President presenting the best all-round athlete award to my brother Joe in 1950.*

man. Brendan taught me to see running as fun and as something to be enjoyed, above everything else. I was to carry this message with me all my competitive life, for I loved to run and race. Crusaders was a wonderful academy for any aspiring athlete, with distinguished international athletes such as Captain Theo Ryan and club officials such as treasurer Louis Vandendries keeping a watchful eye on my progress.

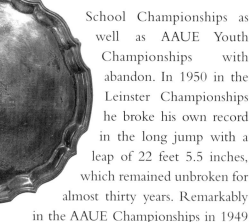

All the while my brother Joe was my real role model and my boyhood hero. I did not start competing in Leinster and Schools competitions until my senior years at Catholic University School. Joe, however,

was an extraordinarily versatile schoolboy athlete, competing for O'Connells at Junior, Intermediate and Senior levels.

In 1946, when I was eleven years old, Joe won the Junior 220 yards title in the Leinster Schools and Colleges Championships. In 1947 as an Intermediate he won the 220 yards title and added the long jump for good measure. Joe's senior years were in 1949 and 1950. He continued to win Leinster and All Ireland

School Championships as well as AAUE Youth Championships with abandon. In 1950 in the Leinster Championships he broke his own record in the long jump with a leap of 22 feet 5.5 inches, which remained unbroken for almost thirty years. Remarkably in the AAUE Championships in 1949 and 1950 he won the Youths' and the Men's long jump titles on the same day as well as the Youths' 220 yards title. To illustrate Joe's versatility, I recall he also won the Leinster 440 yards title (1949) and the AAUE Youths' high jump title (1950). I fondly remember helping Joe to carry home the many prizes he won at the Railway Union sports in Park Avenue when I must have been about fourteen.

Clearly I did not have Joe's talent as a schoolboy. But the pedigree was there; it was first recognised by my maths teacher Jack Sweeney in CUS who encouraged me to enter in the half-mile at the Leinster Colleges Championships in 1952. Mr Sweeney was an accomplished athletics coach at club and university level and among the more distinguished athletes he developed were Irish champions and record-holders Eamon Kinsella, the hurdler, and Brendan O'Reilly, the high jumper. Jack Sweeney's ability to recognise my athletic potential was to set me on my way to becoming an elite athlete a few years later. I might add that I was less successful in my pursuit of higher mathematics with integral calculus proving my downfall!

I was seventeen when I ran my first championship race in the Leinster Colleges in May 1952. You have to picture the scene where there was no specialisation in athletics at schools level. You played rugby for the school from September until you were knocked out of the cup in the spring. Then, if you were good enough, you got on the tennis or cricket team. And in between you might play field hockey for your local club on the 'thirds' or 'fourths'. Tennis and cricket overlapped with athletics, so you really didn't train for athletics as such. Rather you relied on an innate ability to run. Your fitness level was not an issue as your multi-sports participation would have developed your strength and, to a lesser extent, your stamina.

On the 17 May 1952 I got on my bike and cycled from home to the Iveagh Grounds Crumlin to take part in the 880 yards final at the Leinster Colleges Championships. I wore my white cricket flannels, as I did not have a tracksuit. I did have a good pair of spikes, for Dad always ensured we were well equipped to take part in any sport we chose, notwithstanding the difficult financial constraints of the times.

I duly won the Leinster half-mile title and later in the month the All Ireland Colleges title in the Mardyke, Cork. In June I was to win the half-mile at the AAU Youths' Championship and later the All Ireland Youths'. And so ended successfully my first foray into the world of competitive running for another year. Incidentally that summer I also won my first of two Leinster Colleges Tennis Championship medals shoring up the CUS team at No. 6.

What had I learned? Not very much really, except that I could win. I also liked to race and in a perverse way I enjoyed the nervousness of competing and the butterflies in the tummy that went with it. I had experienced for the first time the adrenalin build up prior to racing and, unknowingly, I had experienced its benefits. I was to discover subsequently that this extreme tension was part of the territory. If you wanted to win you had to have the

Above: Leinster Inter-School Lawn Tennis Competition medals. I won in 1952 and 1953, playing for CUS.

Opposite page, bottom: Joe with many of the prizes he won at the Railway Union Sports Day, Park Avenue, summer 1950.

desire. Adrenalin gave you the courage to explore your physical limits irrespective of the pain. In sporting parlance, I was later to learn how to turn the adrenalin on and off like a tap.

My winning times had been ordinary. I didn't exactly rush out and say, 'I must train harder; I must take up athletics seriously'. Instead, I reverted to type, resuming my tennis in Claremont, cricket in Railway and back to school in September until May 1953 when the Schools Championships came around again.

This time Jack Sweeney suggested I should try a 'double' and attempt to win the 880 and 440-yards titles. There was no pressure on me to do so, in fact, my French teacher, Father Tom Lonergan SM, who, like Jack, was involved with the Willwood Foundation in promoting athletics nationally, expressed some concern at the time that I was doing 'too much'!

I tried the double and easily retained my half-mile titles, but came a cropper in the quarter-mile; I finished runner-up to Liam Moloney of Roscrea College, a very good athlete. Liam subsequently could have claimed, if he so wished, that he was the only Irishman ever to beat Ronnie Delany!

By the summer of 1953 I was taking my athletics more seriously and, unlike the previous year, I raced again in July and August. I was eighteen and growing much stronger. I was beginning to enjoy the sheer exhilaration of the race. Tactically, on the advice of Jack Sweeney, I had developed a strategy of making one decisive move in the course of the half-mile race.

The 'decisive move', in simple terms, was to sprint past the leaders at a chosen point from the finish during the last lap. There was an ele-ment of surprise in the tactic which enabled you to gain a few yards lead on your rivals before they reacted and gave chase. It also required confidence and self-belief for this move had to carry you to victory. It carried responsibility too for you were the only one who could take the decision on when to move. Mr Sweeney argued correctly that there was only one such opportunity in the race. There was no such thing as a second decisive move. The 'kick', as it became known, was carrying me to victory each time I ran a half-mile or middle distance race. It was to become the hall-mark of my athletic career later on when honed to perfection in championship racing internationally or around the sharp bends of the board tracks in indoor arenas across the United States.

Again, my times that summer were nothing spectacular. I was winning, but not setting any new records. This was to dramatically change when I was selected by the AAU for a Senior, or Men's, team to compete against the NIAAA in a match race in College Park. I went on to win in a time of 1 minute 58.7 seconds and became the first Irish schoolboy ever to break two minutes for the half-mile. The most telling thing about this achievement was that I now knew I had a very special talent for running. How good I was going to become I had no idea. But instinctively I knew what I had to do. From then on I must specialise in running, give up all my other sports and train as I had never trained before. It was the autumn of 1953 and I would not race again until the following June when I would turn nineteen. I was still only a boy, but I was going to have to explore my every instinct about my true destiny over the coming months. I would make decisions way above my maturity to find out how good an athlete I could be.

The next few months were to prove crucial on two fronts. Firstly, I had to learn how to train for I had never really trained before for athletics as such. My achievements to date were based on a natural talent for running, combined with unusual upper body strength. Secondly, I was to learn that I had been successful in applying for a cadetship in the Irish Army.

It was all very fine for me to decide that I would have to train harder. But the real question was how I should train. It was an amateur era then and no one in Ireland really trained for a specific sport, in the way athletes do today. It was not the done thing. Ask the hard men of rugby from my era.

Change was happening internationally in training techniques and application, especially in running. The legendary Emil Zatopek of Czechoslovakia, in winning multiple gold medals in successive Olympic Games, was beginning to revolutionise attitudes to how hard a man could train. Roger Bannister had intellectualised the art of running in pacing his way to the first four-minute mile.

The new technique was called 'interval training'. I read extensively about it. I wanted to learn more. I learned about it mostly from British sports magazines of the time such as *World Sports* or *Athletics Weekly*. The athletics correspondents, or reporters as they were known, were also writing extensively in the national and international press about this phenomenal new method of interval training. I had to learn more, so I wrote to a leading coach in Britain named David Alford. Coach Alford was a senior Amateur Athletic Association coach, highly qualified and an exponent of the interval system. We began a correspondence course on how I should train using the interval method, which was to carry me through the next year until I went to America. What he recommended certainly worked for me, as I was to find out.

I must have been a curious sight running and jogging seemingly endless intervals round an unmarked grass circuit in the Park Avenue grounds. First I would run a fast segment and then jog a slow segment and recover. I would repeat the sequence until I was exhausted. It is no wonder the watchful and concerned Railway Union alickadoos reportedly said, 'That young fellow will surely kill himself.' But I was not to be deterred. I was pursuing a personal goal with missionary zeal; I was determined to discover the unknown – how good an athlete I could become. It was lonely, too, for I could not share my mission with anyone else in case they thought I was mad. This feeling was to persist for some years. How can you explain your ambition, your dreams when they seem so unlikely?

The second eventuality, winning a cadetship into the Irish Army, was to prove more complex and absolutely test my resolve, my commitment to exploring my athletic talent. Being a cadet seemed, at first, to fit very well into my plans. I would be trained to become an officer with the attendant security of a lifetime career at a time when there were simply no jobs available in an economically-depressed Ireland. And all the while I would have the opportunity to train myself to be a great runner if that was to be my destiny.

With great excitement I enlisted alongside twenty or so classmates into the Irish Army Cadet School at the Curragh, Co. Kildare that December. It did not take me very long to learn that I could not accommodate my twin ambitions to be an officer and an athlete. The military training was going to take absolute precedence and rightly so. In the initial stages sport was something you did at Sports Parade on a Saturday. Later on sports, in particular team sports, would become an integral part of your development.

But I could not wait. It was not possible or acceptable to attempt to pursue further my, by now established, daily training regimen. I had to make a decision. Abandon my ambition to be an athlete or resign from the Cadet School. I opted for the latter, such was my conviction that I was destined to be a great athlete, and immediately sought an honorary discharge from the Army.

To say my father was aghast at the very suggestion that I would leave the Army is putting it mildly. Even though I was very young I had to stand up to him in the most respectful way and convince him that my mind was made up. He could not condone what he considered was a reckless decision on my part. He was right, of course. I was throwing away a lifetime career opportunity on a wild ambition to become the best runner I could possibly be. There was no real logic to what I was proposing to do, other than my own instinct that I was right.

The Minister for Defence duly granted me an honorary discharge and so ended my all too brief army career. In retrospect it is too simple to say I would never have become an Olympic Champion if I had listened to my father. Equally if I had not realised my destiny or lost my commitment I would have felt a sorry fool. But life is full of such complexities and one of the most satisfying memories of my life is being guest of honour of the Chief of Staff at the Army Sports in the Curragh three summers later in 1956, my athletic ambition truly realised by then. I always thought it was a great measure of the mindset of the military in inviting me back to the sports. I felt in a way they were saying – 'Young man we

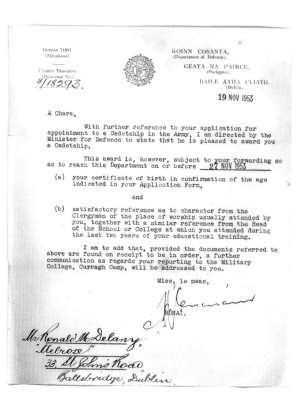

congratulate you. You had the courage of your convictions in pursuing your goal'. In essence, this is what I would have been trained to achieve in life or in conflict if I had remained in the Cadet School.

It was January 1954 and things were not that pleasant living at home in Sandymount. Mammy was great, but Dad was having difficulty coming to terms with what I had done, so recklessly in his mind. Again my option was clear, get out of the house! Dad was always so supportive of me in my pursuit of sporting excellence that it was all the more difficult to go against his wishes. He was the one, after all, who bought me my first tennis racquet and pair of spikes or running shoes. In the depressed economic times of Ireland in the late forties and early fifties there was little or no disposable income available. It must not have been easy for him. I just knew in my own mind I had to do what I was going to do. I had the courage of my convictions then and many times subsequently in my running career.

To be fair, Dad helped me by arranging for me to get an interview for the position of sales representative with Electrolux, selling their well-known vacuum cleaner on a door-to-door basis. I was successful and was appointed as a rep with responsibility for two counties, Carlow and Kilkenny.

I was to be located in Kilkenny and acquired excellent digs with the Misses Coogan in James Street. Dad saw me off to the train at Heuston Station complete with my demonstration Electrolux vacuum cleaner and appendages in a large brown case and of course my upright model bicycle, which was to be my sole means of transport for covering counties Kilkenny and Carlow. That day I left for Kilkenny I think I saw in Daddy's eye a reluctant recognition that his much-loved son was surely intent on pursuing his career come hell or high water. I know I amazed him by my determination, but happily I was never to disappoint him.

My six months in Kilkenny were spent successfully selling vacuum cleaners at night and training with abandon for a few hours each day. Most vacuum cleaner sales were achieved in the evening when the husband was home from work, so my work fitted in well around my training. I was to experience every misadventure that happened to the door-to-door salesman, usually with great hilarity. It was an incredibly happy period of my life. I shared digs with the local teacher, Board of Works engineer, bank clerk and the Singer Sewing Machine sales manager. I enjoyed the high points of the city life, the visiting theatre troupes, exhibitions, cinema, sport and cattle market day, which was something else. I also learned how to sell, a skill that was to remain with me for the rest of my life.

I trained almost daily in James Park on the Freshford Road. There was usually no one there except for a few grazing cattle, wide-eyed bullocks who never quite got used to my antics. I was now applying the interval method of training in my workouts with increasing intensity, as instructed by Coach Alford. The months slipped by. I trained and I worked with enthusiasm, happily merging the two.

During the month of May I sought permission from the Headmaster of St John's College, now Kilkenny College, to use their grass training circuit of about 220 yards. Permission was readily given, not surprisingly I might add, since a previous headmaster of the school was the father of Maeve Kyle née Shankey. Maeve was to be my teammate in Melbourne and represented Ireland in four successive Olympic Games.

This perfectly manicured track was a godsend for I was now able to do speed work in preparation for my first race of the season in the AAU Championships in Dublin. I could not have done more in my preparation. I was ready to race. The day of truth was fast approaching. How much would I have improved? Would it all be worthwhile or had I been living an impossible dream. I would shortly find out the answer.

The date was 11 June 1954. The venue Shelbourne Stadium. The event the 880 yards championship final. I was overlooked by the media in the previews and by my opponents on the day. Included in the small entry was my club mate, the Irish mile champion Michael Byrne, and the much fancied reigning champion R.J. Mackay from Dublin University.

I won the race in a new Irish native record of 1 minute 54.7 seconds, with an electrifying burst of speed on the back straight. The newspapers reported variously that Mackay and Byrne at best could not counter this kind of speed, or at worst that it seemed to leave them standing still.

Four days later I raced again in the Clonliffe Invitational Meeting in College Park. This time, I was racing against international competition for the first time. Visiting teams from the University of Pennsylvania and Cornell were taking part. I won from Paul Raudenbush

(Penn) and Dave Pratt (Cornell) in an exciting race in 1 minute 53.7 seconds improving the previous record by seven-tenths of a second.

My decision to specialise in athletics was clearly vindicated and my instincts for foot racing confirmed. The Delany 'kick' had proven its worth twice against formidable opposition. I now knew that I could race competitively and that I had real athletic talent. This had been my objective for the past year, but it was early days yet. I had no sense of gloating, of saying 'I told you so'. I continued to train hard and raced eight more times before taking part in the European Championships held in Berne, Switzerland in late August 1954.

That is the story of how I learned I was a good runner. I was not an exceptional schoolboy athlete. There was no magic formula. I just had extraordinary self-belief and an unexplainable instinct that this was where my talents lay. This was coupled with an intense dedication to training, and training smart.

Along the way I had demonstrated a decisiveness way beyond my years. Leaving the Cadet School was to prove of paramount importance. But then, how was I to know to do so against my father's advice and almost defying common sense? It was as if I had a mission in life.

It had been a lonely task, training relentlessly in muddy fields and unable to share my ambition with anyone lest I be ridiculed. Loneliness was to prove my constant companion over the next few years as I set out to achieve each daunting goal along the way.

It had not exactly been a barrel of laughs to date. If there were comical moments I was not aware of them. Mick Byrne told me one story some fifty years later about my championship debut in the half-mile against Mackay and himself. He confirmed that they had not even considered me as a threat and thought they had the race sewn up between them. When I kicked past them on the back straight Mick didn't even think I was in the race. He thought I was a sprinter 'warming up', disgracefully mind you, during a Championship final. To his horror when I continued to sprint around the last bend he knew differently.

The night of the Clonliffe International in College Park was a night of opportunity for me, in more ways than one. I spoke afterwards to the Penn Coach, Ken Doherty, who suggested I should explore the opportunity of obtaining an athletic scholarship to an American university. He advised me about the different athletic conferences, which were part of the National Association of Collegiate Athletics (NACA) in the United States. Penn did not issue athletic scholarships at the time, as they were an Ivy League, or privileged, school for the more wealthy Americans. He did name a number of universities on the east and west coasts of America that he thought might be interested in me.

I began to think seriously for the first time about trying for a scholarship. It seemed to make a lot of sense. I could pursue my university education and athletic career at the one time. It would mean leaving Ireland, but then the facilities, coaching and competition in

Breasting the tape, beating Lang Stanley (USA) in a half-mile race at College Park, 4 August 1954

America were the best in the world.

My brother Joe came out of retirement and in late June we scored a Delany double in the All-Ireland Championships. Joe won the long jump and I won the 880 yards. We had fun together competing for Ireland in internationals in London and Cardiff during the summer.

I had done nothing about seeking an athletics scholarship until after a meeting in College Park on the 31 July where I defeated Lang Stanley of the USA. That night I had a fortuitous meeting with Fred Dwyer, a graduate of Villanova University, and an America mile champion. Fred had surprisingly been beaten in the mile by Michael Byrne (Crusaders) earlier in the evening.

Fred told me all about Villanova, about the Irish trailblazers John Joe Barry, Jimmy Reardon

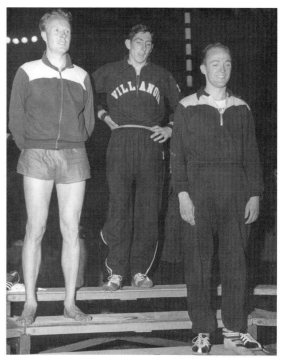

and Cummin Clancy who had gone there following the London Olympics in 1948, and about a coach named 'Jumbo' Elliott.

I was receptive to what Fred Dwyer was telling me about Villanova. I was comfortable with the idea of going over to Mainline Philadelphia to attend a university founded by the Augustine Fathers in 1842 and with such Irish connections. It was the logical thing for me to apply to Villanova with his assistance and advice.

The application process was arduous and thorough and had to be completed in record time. I successfully met the academic requirements and my athletic credentials spoke for themselves. The American Embassy speedily approved my application for a Student or F1 visa after the parish priest from Star of the Sea Church in Sandymount vouched for my good character. Then followed some weeks of frenetic activity to learn in early September that I had been accepted into Villanova on a full athletic scholarship. The decision to try my luck in America had proven a lot easier than my decision to leave the Irish Army. But I was not exactly sure what was facing me.

Looking back at that time, at my journey into the unknown, my life at the university, I remember how my athletic career took off beyond my wildest expectations, how I constantly set and re-set my goals, building success on success, culminating in my Olympic victory in the 1,500-metre final in Melbourne.

I was now travelling to Villanova more in expectation than in hope, for in the European Championships in late August I had gained a new status and growing confidence. A three-man Irish team travelled to compete in Berne – Eamon Kinsella in the 110m hurdles and Brendan O'Reilly in the high jump. I was to compete in the 800 metres. In round one, heat 4 I ran a new national record of 1 minute 51.8 seconds. Two days

Bon Voyage

RONNIE DELANEY, dual Irish record holder in the half mile (1 min. 50 secs.) and mile (4 mins. 5.8 secs.), leaves Ireland on Wednesday for Villanova University, U.S.A. where he will continue his studies (commerce and finance).

Ronnie can well feel satisfied with his visit home as he returned his best time ever for the half mile and mile and proved himself a runner of world class. But his capabilities are, to a large extent, still unknown, as the manner in which he broke the Irish mile record on August 5 seems to be only a preview of better things to come.

Will he be home again next year? "At present I am unable to say, but if at all possible I will. I aim to continue running over both the half mile and mile, and will do my best to improve on my figures of this year."

At twenty years of age, Ronnie's successes have been little short of phenomenal. Billy Morton, who has been responsible in no small way for Ronnie's successes, told me: "After seeing Ronnie run over the '880' and mile, I am convinced that his best distance is the 1,500 metres, and would even go as far as to say that if he runs in this distance at Melbourne next year, he will win an Olympic gold medal.".

Yes, this soft-spoken young man, who resides in Sandymount, Dublin, has certainly given Irish athletics a great 'fillip,' and I am sure that I express the sentiments of all Irish sportsmen when I say 'bon voyage, Ronnie.'

B. H.

Telegramm – Télégramme – Telegramma

HEARTIEST CONGRATULATIONS KEEP GOOD WORK UP = UNCLE JOE +

ELT = RONNIE DELANEY C/O IRISH TEAM EUROPEAN ATHLETIC CHAMPIONSHIP BERNE =

later, in the first semi-final, I broke my record when finishing second in 1 minute 50.2 seconds. The next day, emotionally drained and exhausted, I finished last in the final in two minutes plus. I was now competitive at championship level. I was no longer just a promising young athlete. I could take on the best middle distance runners in the world, albeit with fear and trepidation! I could now realistically expect to win races, to suffer defeats, of course, to learn from victory and defeat and hopefully I could expect to take part in the Melbourne Olympic Games, a little over two years away.

Opposite page, top: On the winners' podium after my first 4-minute mile in Compton, CA, 1 June 1956, with (l-r) Gunnar Nielsen (Denmark) and Fred Dwyer (Villanova).

Opposite page, bottom: Villanova track coach 'Jumbo' Elliott, stopwatch in hand.

This page, left: With Eamon Kinsella and Brendan O'Reilly at the European Championships, Berne, Switzerland, 1954.

THE ALL-AMERICAN BOY

I began to write about my time in America as a scholarship athlete some time during the autumn of 1967. I thought my story would appeal to an American readership. It was an adventure story in the classic mould of 'Irish lad makes good in the land of opportunity'. It was insightful for I was writing about a whole new world from the perspective of a young Irishman who had just emigrated from his native country, a land of little opportunity in the fifties. But this young man had a dream – he wanted to be one of the best athletes in the world.

I submitted the text to the publishers of *Sports Illustrated*, the leading sports magazine in America, enjoying even then a massive circulation and readership. Time Inc. responded enthusiastically and before I had time to blink, let alone think, I had signed a very remunerative contract to have my story published over two issues of the magazine in January 1968. I had no difficulty completing the story to meet their deadlines in early December. I was after all writing from the heart with most of the detail still fresh in my memory.

The articles reproduced in these chapters cover the years from my arrival at Villanova up to my Olympic win.

The need to earn a few dollars was also a strong motivating factor. My wife Joan and I were blessed with three beautiful children at the time, Lisa, Ronnie and Jennifer, and the various bills had accumulated. Christmas 1967 was going to be great for we were solvent for the first time in our young married life. You can only imagine our excitement on Christmas Eve when we learned by airmail letter from Time Inc. that they had decided to run my story over three issues of the magazine. In accordance with our agreement they enclosed a further cheque in final payment. We hugged and danced around the hall with the children looking on in bewilderment. Our

joy and our family were completed the next year when our beautiful daughter Michelle came along.

RUNNING OF THE GREEN

First printed in *Sports Illustrated*, January 15, 1968

Winter means something different to everyone. Now that I have given up running round in circles, winter holds a very special significance for me. I retired from athletics some years ago, 1962 to be exact, and retired to Ireland in a different sense even before then, in 1960. I came home that year to my first love, Dublin, to settle down. I lived at home for a while, then did my bit to ruin the late marrying trend in the country by getting wed at the early age of twenty-seven years. I have my own home, a loving and patient wife and three potential Olympians of my own.

But back to winter. When I was living in America, winter meant the indoor season, a round of races spread from New York to Boston, Milwaukee, Philadelphia, Cleveland and Chicago,

from January through March. Winter's Fridays or Saturdays from 1955 to 1959 were no ordinary days. I donned the Villanova singlet and stepped out on a board track to race for college and country against the cream of the world's athletes. Tension, excitement, thrills were there in plenty – and they are still with me, every bit as alive today. Almost with my first breath of cold January air my mind flashes back through the years and I can smell the wooden chips off the board tracks of many an arena. Without closing my eyes I'm back in Madison Square Garden and I can hear the crowd. Mixed emotions.

This page: Showing off the medal for a photo call at home with Jennifer (in my arms), Ronnie & Lisa.

Opposite, bottom: With my team-mate and friend, Alex Breckenridge in the Villanova field house, 1956.

Some cigar-chewing, beer-drinking fanatic perched up near the rafters screams down at me, 'Delany, you bum, when are you goin' to run?' or the tumultuous cheers of that same crowd after I had for once 'run' and perhaps set a new world indoor mark for the mile.

My youngest daughter, Michelle.

But it all began long before – September 23, 1954, and I was at Shannon Airport ready to board a Pan American flight to the States to avail myself of an athletic scholarship at Villanova University. I was emotionally drained and upset at leaving my mother and father. I kissed them goodbye and for all I knew would never see them again. And I was leaving, too, my beloved Ireland.

Things had happened so fast. A few letters to Villanova. A cable telling me I was accepted as a scholarship student from Coach Jumbo Elliott. The mad hustle to secure my airline ticket and visa, a new suit of clothes – and where was Villanova? I didn't even know. Would anyone meet me?

In New York I was one of the last off the aircraft, and as I stepped out into the sweltering September heat I was almost overcome by the belt of warm, humid air. My tweed suit and woollen under-wear, coupled with the load of hand pieces I had to haul, made me soon wonder if I had stepped into another country or a Turkish bath. I still did not know where Villanova was. I asked a few people but no one seemed to know.

Just then I saw a handsome

young man on the other side of a rampart, wearing a large blue sweater with a big white 'V' on it. For the first time, and without realising it, I uttered the college cheer, 'V for Villanova', and gathering my bits and pieces made straight over to him with the most relieved smile of my life lighting my face. He was Jim Moran, captain of the Villanova track team, and he had come up to New York to collect me. And I might add, thanks be to God, for if I were left on my own I would probably never have found the place and might have ended up in Manhattan College.

We still had to journey into New York City, take a train to Philadelphia and from there the P & W out the Main Line to Villanova. Jim must have realised how tired I was, for all the while he avoided my questions about how far it was to the college. 'Another few minutes,' he kept reassuring me. I fell asleep for the whole journey from New York to Philadelphia, but by then my excitement at the prospect of seeing the Villanova campus carried me on the last stage to my new home.

And I was not disappointed. My first impression of the university was one of amazement at the size of the place – so many different buildings, all of which I was soon to know – and at the beauty of the campus. Rolling green hills, over which I was to jog many a mile, stretched as far as my eye could see. I was delighted. I felt I was going to be happy in America.

Perhaps the most welcome sight after all my journeying was a wire-spring bed in Jim Moran's room. I lay myself down to sleep, and sleep I did. I have it on good report I slept well over twenty-four hours straight. In fact, while asleep, without knowing it, I was achieving some notoriety. The track team and Coach Elliott began to wonder what sort of athlete they had got themselves. 'Hell, is this Irishman going to sleep all day, every day?'

Much to their surprise, I eventually got up, and then began the process of meeting a myriad of new faces, some of whom would be my closest friends for the next five years. Al Ligorelli, Johnny Kopil, George Browne, Charlie Jenkins, Bill Rock, Alex Breckenridge, to name but a few, met me and welcomed me to Villanova. Everyone was so friendly I could hardly believe it. And everything about America was so new to me I had not a moment to be homesick. The cars, such colours, size and style; no longer pictures in a magazine but roaring by me down Lancaster Avenue. The first time I walked across the campus, everywhere I looked I saw squirrels scampering beneath the trees or brazenly seeking tidbits from the passersby. I had never seen a squirrel before.

The food was strange at first, but such quantity. The snazzy clothes the students wore – my old tweed suit, I'm sure, looked a little out of place. White bucks and chinos – soon I'd be sporting them myself. Hot dogs and hoagies and twenty-nine flavours of ice cream. The New World was more exciting than I ever dreamed.

Within a few days I had duly registered in the School of Commerce and Finance, got myself a room in Mendel Hall, and begun to attend lectures. I was delighted to find that my fellow students had a sense of humour, though perhaps a tendency to disrespect authority. Before the official class registers came out we had to sign a roll sheet at each lecture. Without fail some jokers would sign bogus names, such as Frank Sinatra, Elvis Presley or Martin Luther. When the professor read out the roll it never failed to get a laugh. However, I did not notice him smiling. He'd obviously gone through the routine before.

Outside the tuckshop on the Villanova campus with team-mates (l-r) Johnny Kopil, Joe Mannion, Vic Di Maio and George Browne.

Coach Elliott impressed on me the need to hit the books during my first few weeks at Villanova. This was one of the many fine pieces of advice he was to give me while I was under his direction. He seemed more concerned that I should study than train. He asked me to report to the track only three days a week.

I did not realise how astute a judge of an athlete Jumbo was the first time I worked out under his care. After seeing me run a few laps he took me aside and gave me some critical advice on my arm action ('too jerky'), head ('rolls too much') and shoulders ('too stooped'). Listening to him I began to wonder how I had managed to run at all up to then with all my deformities. Naturally I was enraged, but I kept my mouth

The start of the 1,000 yards at the Philadelphia Enquirer Games, 1955 (Tom Courtney, 1956 Olympic 800-metre champion is on my right.)

shut. Yet somewhere in between all the criticism Jumbo said, 'You'll make a miler.' I was sceptical, for I had never run a mile in my life. Little did I realise that with Jumbo's care and guidance I would become a miler and an Olympic 1,500-metre champion at that.

At first I took no part in the social life at the college. Basically, I was a very shy person. I was easily embarrassed, particularly in the company of girls. There were not many girls in the college – though we had a nursing school – and most of the lads described coeds as dogs. Pretty girls were at a premium and were quickly snapped up by the men about campus. Still, any of the girls I met seemed friendly, though very sophisticated, too much so for the tastes of a simple Irish lad. I remember being introduced to a girl one day as I crossed Mendel Field. When she learned I was from Ireland she said, 'Please say something.' I think she expected me to sound like Barry Fitzgerald. Later I came to realise that people liked my Irish brogue even if they complained they could not understand me. Remarks such as, 'Hey, Mick, take the potatoes out of your mouth so I can understand you,' at first offended me, but then I learned that this sort of ribbing was intended as friendly. Coach Elliott rightly pointed out to me that if people didn't like you they would say nothing to you at all. Before long I was answering back the remarks with a repartee of my own – sometimes with interest, I might add.

Caddying at Overbrook Golf club – carrying two bags was hard work.

It did not take me too long to realise the almighty power of the dollar. Jim Moran took me caddying one day to the Radnor Valley Country Club. I got out, and after carrying two giant bags for 18 holes I was paid $5 and given a dollar tip by the golfers, certainly not for giving them the right clubs. Never having played golf before, or ever caddied, I was as likely to produce the putter on the tee and the driver on the green. But $6 – I was rich. Every day that I didn't have to train, and on weekends, too, I hared off to Radnor or the Overbrook Golf Club and caddied for some misfortunate golfers. I enjoyed the exercise, the fresh air and the money.

Hurricane Hazel became another source of income. I spent many weeks cutting up fallen trees for local people – at a dollar an hour. I also branched out into the babysitting business at 50 cent an hour. And painting, household repairs, car waxing, gardening — you name it, I did it. I was becoming a regular tycoon.

Minding Coach Elliott's children at home (l-r) Joy, Jimmy, Geoff and Tommy.

One night I was working at the field house as a parking attendant. There was a big affair going on, and all sorts of dignitaries were arriving. A sleek black giant of a Cadillac drove up to the steps of the field house and this tall, distinguished-looking gentleman stepped out and announced himself to me as 'Farley, New York.' Taking his outstretched hand I replied, 'Delany, Dublin, Ireland.' We engaged in a short, friendly chat. You can imagine my amazement when I learned afterward that I had been talking to the ex-Postmaster General of the United States, the Honourable James A. Farley.

In November, approximately two months after my arrival in the US, I travelled to New York for my first race in the Villanova colours. Jumbo Elliott entered me in the freshman three-mile cross-country race for the Intercollegiate AAAA Championships, held in Van Cortlandt Park. It was a big occasion for me and I was anxious to do well. I had never run a cross-country race in my life. Van Cortlandt Park's terrain was as dry and as hard as a bone on that particular November day. It was a far cry from the green, green grass of home. And cross-country, my eye! The course ran across the hard-packed plains of the park, along bridle paths, up the sides of rocky hills, across public roads, in and out between the trees, where one false step meant an abrupt *finis*, and eventually back on the plains again for a long run into the finishing tape. At the start we were stretched out in a great line across the park, and then the starter raised his arm and fired the gun. Displaying more heart than pace sense, I stayed up with the leaders in the early stages and was soon caught up in the exhilaration of it all. I felt as though I were participating on foot in the Charge of the Light Brigade.

With 'Jumbo' Elliott after Villanova won the IC4A Championship in 1958.

But my fancy thoughts were unceremoniously knocked out of me as we reached the first turn. In the 'squeeze in' for position I tasted for the first time the sharp elbows of my American opponents. And educated elbows they had, too. After receiving two or three strategic belts in the ribs, I realised this was war. I was facing the most competitive nation in the world ... a factor that would provide me with thrilling competition in many a race for the next five years, indoors and out.

Realising immediately my shortcomings in the adept art of infighting, I resolved to keep out of arms' reach for the remainder of the course. After covering a mile and a half of the three-mile course, I found myself in the lead. I ran on happily, opening a wide gap between myself and the trailing pack. My biggest problem at this stage was to keep on the right course. There were all sorts of arrows to follow, on the sides of trees and painted on the ground. Madly waving officials were there at every cross point to ensure you took the right turn. With their help and my 20-20 vision I found my way home to the finishing line, a 75-yard victor over Michael Midler of Cornell. I had made a promising start to my racing career in America. I only hoped and prayed I would have the ability to keep it up.

Returning to Villanova, I successfully completed midterm exams ... not brilliantly mind you, but sufficiently to augur well for the future. Accounting and English literature were giving me some trouble. Our English professor was a rather sophisticated type and we met head on once or twice. He severely criticised me publicly one day, much to the amusement of my classmates, for borrowing Longfellow's words, 'footprints on the sands of time', and using them in an essay assignment. I rose, as would any friend of Longfellow's, to defend the value of his metaphor. The professor was not impressed and accused me of having kissed the Blarney stone. But I never had!

In early December I got my first glimpse of an indoor running track, though outdoors. The board track had been laid out in the Villanova

With Coach Elliott at his desk in the Track Office, Villanova Field House, 1954.

Stadium. It was a strange-looking thing with steeply banked corners and short straightaways, 12 laps to the mile. If it was odd to look at, I was to find it even more peculiar to run on at first.

The first time I tried to negotiate a turn at speed I went right up on the bank to the outside board. But with expert coaching and the advice of my friend and teammate, Charlie Jenkins, I was soon negotiating the turns like a veter-an. Jumbo called me a natural and assured me I would have no prob-lems adjusting my stride to the tighter board circuit.

The whole atmosphere toward training had now changed. With the opening of the indoor season looming up in early January, there was a seriousness about the workouts. We trained every day and trained hard. Jumbo's rallying call was no longer 'hit the books' but 'hit the track'. And this we did, varsity and freshmen. Dedication and determination were evident in the approach of each athlete – the type of approach that had made America the greatest power in the world in track and was to make the comparatively small Villanova squad the greatest college track team in America for the next five years. Intercollegiate championships, indoors and out, National Collegiate championships, world records, Olympic titles were the prizes at stake. There was no room for shirking, no easy way to the top.

I was caught up in this atmosphere. It was something completely new to me. My blood was fired with a new enthusiasm. I relished the exhausting workouts – the harder the better. I was not alone. I was one of many young men reaching for the sky. The outdoor elements, rain or snow, did not deter us. There was a job to be done and we were about to do it well. Jumbo impressed on us the value of our efforts, of each monotonous mile pounded out on the creaking board track in the Villanova Stadium. 'Money in the bank' was how he described it, an investment in our running futures. 'Train hard and the races will take care of themselves' was the motto he gave us. None of us stopped to question him, and for the first time in my life I knew what it felt to be part of a team. I was still an Irishman, and would always be, but gradually I was becoming a Villanovan. In future I would race with a double purpose, for the honour of Ireland and for Villanova. I already felt I belonged in the dynamic world of American track and field. I was determined to make a worthwhile contribution.

That December began what was to be a lasting friendship with Charlie Jenkins, Villanova's Olympic 400-metre champion at Melbourne. Despite my outwardly friendly disposition I did not make friends easily, and never have to this day. Perhaps it was the individual nature of athletics, the amount of dedication required, the tension that was constantly there, if mostly beneath the surface, but I had always been somewhat of a loner. The self-discipline one imposed on oneself did not exactly make one the life and soul of a party. It was impossible to share your feelings with someone who did not understand the very nature of your sport. Friendship, too, probably required an amount of giving, and this I was not prepared to do. All the giving I was prepared to make was concentrated in the one area – toward making me a champion.

With my fellow Olympic Champion and friend Charles Jenkins who won the 400 metres and a relay gold (4x400m) in Melbourne.

My friendship with Charlie was different. Our objectives were the same, and we were driven on by the same ambition. We worked together in training, pushing each other to the limits of our endurance. We helped each other in time trials and by critical advice. We were of the same mould. The similarity of our makeup and our closeness on the track led to a truly great friendship that I will treasure for the rest of my life. We began to share our personal problems and ideas with each other off the track, too. Religion and girl friends became our two favourite topics for conversation. Later on, when the competitive season started, on pre-race days we took long walks out along the country roads near

Villanova and plotted the tactics for the downfall of an opponent. Charlie was an articulate public speaker and we shared many a top dais at Communion breakfasts, sports banquets and other functions. Here, too, we competed against each other – with witticisms and funny stories, our prize not so much the applause of the audience but one-upmanship on each other.

While my approach to athletics changed that first December in Villanova, life had not suddenly become all serious. There was still room for many a lighter moment. All was not dull or dedication. The Christmas vacation came around and I decided to stay on campus with another foreigner, Alex Breckenridge from Glasgow, Scotland, for company. Alex was a two-miler and eventually was to represent the US in the marathon at the Rome Olympics. Mr Elliott employed us for the holiday in the company he worked for then, Franz Equipment Co. Ltd., in what capacity I do not know to this day. I think we were the funniest thing to happen along for the workers in Franz Equipment for many a year. The first morning we reported for duty we were shown out to the plant, where we met a foreman called Sam. It was obvious from the start that Sam and the boys were out to have some fun at our expense. They were openly amused by our accents, Breckenridge's burr and my brogue. The first job we were given to do involved measuring yards and yards of steel cable. Sam gave us a ruler about three feet long and told us to get on with the job. We must have made quite a sight, rolling out hundreds of yards of steel cable and proceeding to measure the lot with a ridiculous three-foot ruler. To add to our troubles we were working out of doors, and I had never experienced such cold weather in all my life.

After two or three days we realised the futility of it all, so we devised a formula for measuring the length of the cables without even having to unravel them. I hope to this day that no crane mechanic ever used our measured cables in his work without checking the length first. I shudder to think what the consequences could have been. Still, we survived the elements and were paid a salary for our efforts at the end of it all. After taxes we took home about $75 each, more money than I had ever had in my life. We had a happy Christmas.

Shortly after Christmas the track team members returned to Villanova, cutting short their vacations, to complete preparations for our first indoor meet, the Knights of Columbus Games in Boston. Coach Elliott informed me I was entered in the Bishop Cheverus Memorial 1,000-Yard Run. I had never raced at the distance before, but this did not worry me unduly. My main worry was that I had never raced on the boards before. Sure, I was doing well in training and had just completed a confidence-building half-mile time trial on the Villanova boards. But training and racing were two different things.

Saturday, January 15, crept up on me and I found myself in the lobby of the Manger Hotel, Boston, on the day of my indoor debut. The nervous tension associated with competing was beginning to build up. I was trying to control it and to remain as complacent as possible under the circumstances. Outwardly I probably appeared calm but inside me a volcano of nervous energy was slowly turning over. One moment I was full of doubts – doubting my own ability, my fitness and my purpose. Then I would reassure myself that I was capable of beating my opponents, analysing and comparing their past performances with my own.

It was mid-afternoon and I had not yet seen the indoor track laid out in the Boston Garden. More precisely, I had never been inside an indoor arena in my life. Boston was Charlie Jenkins' home town and we had arranged that he would show me the Garden. We went over and Charlie gave me a right Cook's Tour, pointing out the dressing rooms, the best areas for warming up and the starting and finishing lines on the track for the 1,000-yard. The arena itself was vast and frightening, with towering seats on all sides stretching right up to the roof. But looking up at the empty seats I was conscious, too, of the intimacy of the place. I suddenly felt lonely, for I realised that every face staring down from those same seats later that evening would be unknown to me. I was a stranger and terribly alone. Returning to the hotel, I retired to my room to rest and prepare myself mentally. I resigned myself stoically to the task at hand. There was no escape now. My concentration was intense and I was determined to run to the best of my ability.

I went over to the Garden and to the Villanova dressing room without even taking a glimpse inside at the crowded arena. While changing into the Villanova colours I could hear the roar of the crowd somewhere in the background. I began to sense and feel for the first time the excitement of indoor track. Little did I realise then how big a part this new sport I was about to sample would play in my athletic career for the next five years.

I moved out into the passageways circling the arena beneath the seating and began my warm-up. This took some doing. The passages were full of people moving to and fro between the hot dog stands, beer counters, conveniences, and their seats. They were a good-humoured crowd and while downing their beers and stuffing themselves with hot dogs they shouted words of encouragement to the runners trotting by. They did not seem to appreciate that the athletes were trying to warm up for their races; they stopped whomever they liked for his autograph. No one knew me, and I was not bothered at all.

One side of the arena was quieter than the other, so I began to do some fast strides along the 60 yards or so of passageway. As I was striding along at full speed, an oversize gent stepped out of a stairway straight in my path. My running career almost came to a premature end at that moment, but I managed to glance off him with no damage, save the loss of my friend's beer, much to his disgust. I can't recall exactly what he shouted after me, but he certainly wasn't wishing me good luck.

It was time now to move inside to the arena for the race. I remember feeling reasonably calm under the circumstances as I sat down in the centre of the arena to put on my spiked shoes. Looking up into the crowd I could see a sea of faces, all unfamiliar. I felt a sudden jolt as the announcer called for 'all competitors in the 1,000-yard run.' This was the moment I had trained for.

I stepped out on the board track to run the first indoor race of my life. As each competitor was announced he trotted forward, waved his hand in greeting to the cheer of the crowd and then went back to the starting line. For some strange reason or other there was a separate spotlight beaming on me all the time. I had no time then to figure out why but after the race I learned that the assistant electrician in the Boston Garden was a countryman of mine, Joe Casey. He was doing his bit to put some steel into my soul for the race ahead.

The race began and it was like a nightmare. I tried to secure a good position at the first bend but a sturdy favourite of the Garden crowd, Carl Joyce, unceremoniously belted me aside as he came up on my inside. Every time I moved up alongside a runner I got the same treatment. Biff, bang, wallop – I wondered if this was boxing or track. Somehow or other I managed to get to the front, about 100 yards from the finish, with Lang Stanley and Gene Maynard, the Big Ten champion, breathing down my neck. It was the safest place to be and I edged my way to the finish, a winner in the new track record time of 2:10.2.

Exhausted but truly delighted by my success, I made my way slowly around the outside of the track catching my breath and still spotlighted by Joe Casey, this time in a green light. The crowd was giving me a great reception and I began to realise what people meant when they said Boston was a real Irish town. Jumbo came up to me, shook my hand and said well done. In the next breath he said, 'Boy, have you got a lot to learn.' I knew what he meant, for in winning I had never taken such a beating in all my life. I would have to learn how to take care of myself on the boards.

I learned well, for I never lost a race in the Boston Garden. And, after two losing races elsewhere that winter, I was for five years to run undefeated indoors. Those years are a mixture of memories – happy, sad, at times confusing. A winner but subjected to the boos of the crowd, crossing swords with officials and as a result threatened with suspension for life, more roughhouse tactics on the track, integrating myself socially into the American way of life, romance, aspiring to be an actor – these were all a part of the next five years.

Boston Evening Globe

Sports

WEDNESDAY, JANUARY 14, 1959   Forty-Three

HABIT-FORMING—

Delany Shoots For 29 Straight

By JERRY NASON

To appreciate what a footsy fellow Herb Elliott the Aussie is you merely have to recall that Ron Delany can't beat him in running a mile.

Yet Delany, in this town, rates up there with Paul Revere, Clarence DeMar and Brass Monkey among famous perambulators.

The Irish laddy returns to the scene of his original American triumph on Saturday evening—K. of C. meet, Boston Garden.

Having been adrift from the sports beat hereabouts for a week we are not too familiar with the opposition which they've assembled to face him.

DELANY

Unless they've come up with Elliott himself it doesn't figure to make much difference.

The thing that may make a difference in Delany this year is that he no longer is exposed to the undergraduate scene. As a graduate student his training becomes more a matter of self-discipline.

Some, like Glenn Cunningham, respond to it, make the personal sacrifices necessary to the training routine. Others, like Bill Bonthron, cannot justify the effort with the results attained.

In the trade they feel that Delany will excel as a graduate miler because of his devotion to miling's competitive aspects.

Defense of his Olympic 1500 meters title has been a goal, if not an obsession with him.

Such a goal would keep him in competition through August, 1960 . . . and, needless to say, a top drawer miler today cannot afford a falloff in training.

The world competition is too good . . . Elliott, Hewson, Waern, Ibbotson, Orywal and at least a half dozen other fly boys pointing for Rome—and at Delany.

Boston appreciates the stutter-sprinting Delany probably as much as his native Dublin. His first American conquest was scored here (K. of C. 1000, 1955) and the local shilalagh set made him president of the club long ago.

It has become overlooked in the confusion that rapid Ronnie has won 28 consecutive indoor races—24 of them in the mile.

Either streak is a record for the boards, as is the 4:02.4 mile mark which he was compelled to unveil at Chicago last March.

The average track addict can't recall the only defeats Delany has ever sustained in board-track running . . . although they were in the '55 season to Norway's Audun Boysen and Arnie Sowell at shorter distances.

Another nice thing that Boston promoters like about Ron Delany is that he sells tickets . . .

Left: In my role as Colonel Pickering in G.B. Shaw's Pygmalion, *Rosemount College, November 1958.*

MAKER OF MILERS

HOW I BECAME A MILER:
THE APPRENTICESHIP

First printed in *Sports Illustrated*, January 22, 1968

Ireland's Olympic champion-to-be was advised by his shrewd coach, Jumbo Elliott, 'Hold your elbows high and ready.' Victory came easily on crowded indoor tracks, but when the campaign went outdoors Delany had to learn harsh lessons about pace and technique.

There was no celebration after my first victory indoors in the Knights of Columbus Games in Boston. We had to catch the midnight train back to Philadelphia. I would have enjoyed going out on the town now that the tension associated with the race was gone. Instead I found myself stretched out in a Pullman sleeper, alone with my thoughts. After a hard race I could never go to sleep – my body tingled in every muscle from the exertion undergone. So I spent the night awake listening to the clickety-clack of the wheels and the jangling of milk churns being loaded on and off the train at almost every station stop. On Monday, back at Villanova, I reported as usual for training. Coach Jumbo Elliott took me aside and spent the afternoon schooling me on how to protect myself in my future races on the boards. My eyes were opened! I discovered if you must push an opponent there was no better place than at hip level where you could most readily upset his equilibrium. 'Hold your elbows high and ready when you are being crowded' was another trick of the trade. It was a revelation to me, for I did not realise there was an art to self-defence and the administration of punishment when provoked on the track. Knowledge such as this was to help me through the preliminary heats of Olympic Games, European championships and other title races over the next few years. I was learning my trade well.

I raced again the following Friday night in the Borican 1,000 yards at the *Philadelphia Inquirer* meet and won in a pedestrian 2:15.5, with Tom Courtney and Harry Bright among my victims. Courtney was to win the Melbourne Olympic 800 metres in 1956 and we were to engage in an almost vicious rivalry over the next few years. Tom hated to be beaten, and much to his disgust I did just that to him almost

51

every time we raced. A year or so after we both retired from active competition I met Tom at a B'nai B'rith dinner in New York. He spent the night moaning that I had beaten him on the last occasion we had raced, in Houston, Texas, and that he had never had an opportunity for revenge. I believe if we could have borrowed running vests and shorts on that same evening Tom would have challenged me to come outside and race along a few blocks of New York City to prove to himself that he was the better man.

Following the *Inquirer* meet I had my first dispute with Coach Elliott. I discovered that he had put me down to run again in the Millrose Games half mile a week or so later. It appeared I was going to have to race every weekend throughout the winter. Frankly, I felt I was being rushed and brought on too fast. I felt then this American system of race, race, race would burn me out. I wanted to run my best races for Ireland in her green international singlet and not to leave my talent and strength in the smoke-filled indoor arenas of America. I expressed such sentiments to Jumbo. He nearly blew his top. Somewhere between his threats and shouts I gathered I would run where and when I was told, or else. The 'else' meant, I supposed, losing my scholarship. I lost this first argument with Jumbo, setting the pattern for the next five years, and ran in the Millrose Games. But I have no regrets. Racing every weekend did me no harm but made me strong. Even today I am grateful to Jumbo for what at the time seemed like coercing me into running. I discovered, too that the life of an athletic scholarship student was not going to be a bed of roses – the college demanded and got its pound of flesh.

In the Millrose Games half mile in Madison Square Garden I suffered my first defeat in America, at the hands – or should I say feet – of Audun Boysen of Norway. The Madison Square Garden atmosphere was different from either Boston or Philadelphia – more exciting altogether. The crowd of 15,000 was discerning and far more vociferous. As I warmed up in the passages circling the arena I sensed the electric tension of the place and felt like a lion awaiting his entrance into the ancient circuses of Rome. Later I was to discover that this crowd of New York track nuts almost needed blood to be sated. And later still, when I began to run and win miles week after week, in far from world-shattering times, I believe these same fans would have strangled me on occasions if they had got half a chance. My relationship with the New York buffs was to be a turbulent affair with very little love on either side.

The race itself was a scorcher. Boysen ran a meet record of 1:51 flat and I struggled home in second place 15 yards down. Courtney, Gene Maynard, Harry Bright and company brought up the rear. Disappointed though I was, I had to laugh afterward. In my innocence, while in the dressing room with Boysen prior to the race, I had asked him if he were fit. Answering me in his best broken English, Boysen explained that he had no opportunity to train in snow-covered Norway, that he had a sore leg, etc., etc. And then look at what he did to me. I was discovering that to be a great runner you also had to be a pathological liar, at least when your opponents asked silly questions.

On February 19, 1955 I travelled again to New York to compete in the AAU Championships. I suffered another reverse, finishing fourth in the 1,000 yards to Arnold Sowell of Pittsburgh. Yet I had the honour of competing in a world record race, for Sowell beat Boysen and ran 2:08.2 to equal the existing world best. Unfortunately though, Tom Courtney, who was third, finished ahead of me for the first time, rubbing salt into my wounds.

With all this racing, and with midterm exams coming up, there was no time to even consider pursuing the social round. My many dollar-earning enterprises were also affected and I was reduced to baby-sitting as a sole source of income. But the indoor season was almost over. A week later I anchored the Villanova Frosh to win the IC4A distance medley in New York, running a mile for the first time in my life. I have forgotten what time I ran and my only recollection of the race is how strange I felt running the longer distance. I didn't particularly enjoy my first mile outing.

On March 5, the day before my 20th birthday, I celebrated with a victory in the Cardinal McIntyre 1,000-yard run, again in Madison Square Garden. This race was the finale of my first indoor season. I bobbed and turkey-trotted, as the scribes would say, to victory in a new meet mark of 2:10.1, with Tom Courtney breathing down my neck to the wire. I had my first date after the meet, doubling with Alex Breckenridge of Scotland and two girls from Rosemont College near Villanova. When a Scot and an Irishman go out on the town they really do things big. We dined the girls at Horn & Hardart's – the Automat – and spent the rest of the week ruing our spendthriftiness. Still, we had fun and, more important, I had broken the ice and had taken out an American girl.

I was generally relieved that the indoor season was over and spring was on the way. Racing every weekend, combined with the travelling involved, had proved gruelling. Training on the Villanova board track out of doors in the freezing cold was not the most pleasant way to pass one's leisure hours. Some days we had to grease our faces and ears with Vaseline to protect them from the cold. We must have looked quite a sight wearing long johns and hooded anoraks, our faces covered with grease and sweat, charging around the track.

The freshman squad ran in very few meets during the outdoor season. Coach Elliott did not require us to train hard or on a regular basis, so I had a chance to get in some extra study. I had the opportunity also to observe American youth enjoying its own particular version of the riot of spring. I was amazed. With the coming of the first warm days the boys on campus went wild and headed straight for the nearest girls' school. There appeared to be one mad round of picnics and beer-drinking parties. It was as if they had been caged all winter and suddenly let loose on the world or, should I say, the girls. It was very hard to keep one's mind on running with all the courting going on. But gradually things simmered down and my roommate and the rest returned to normal, I assume from sheer exhaustion.

I had one important race outdoors, an invitation half mile in the Coliseum Relays in Los Angeles. A star-studded field was mustered including Mal Whitfield, the reigning and twice Olympic champion; Lon Spurrier, world record holder at the distance; Arnie Sowell; Lang Stanley and, my old foe by now, Tom Courtney. It was to be the toughest race of my life so far. I felt I was only a boy. I had read about the legendary Whitfield in the '48 and '52 Olympics and here I was in a race competing against him. But reputations count for naught, as I

Right: Hamming it up on the outdoor board track, NYU, Manhattan, while training for the indoor relay season, 1962. (L-r) Derek McCleane, Tom O'Riordan and Basil Clifford.

was soon to discover. The race itself was a real dogfight from the gun with elbows and fists flying as fast as our feet. In the final lap Sowell was knocked clean off the track. Courtney finished first and I was second, with Spurrier, Stanley and Whitfield running up in that order. But Tom was disqualified for cutting in on Sowell on the final bend and I was declared the winner.

Tom shrieked 'highway robbery' and in my opinion rightly so. He should never have been disqualified, for he did no more wrong than anyone else. We should all have been disqualified for one of the dirtiest races of all time.

A few days after this race a letter came from Billy Morton, the athletics impresario of Ireland, enclosing tickets for me to travel home to compete in some races for him during the summer. I was overjoyed. It was not that I was unhappy in America. I had made many friends and I was well settled in at Villanova. But I was thrilled at the prospect of getting home again so soon. I was flattered, too, to think that an athletic promoter felt it worth his while to incur the expense of bringing me home to race before the Irish crowds. Before I knew it, end-of-term exams were completed, successfully I hoped, and I was on my way

Playing the piano at home prior to my departure for Villanova, September 1954.

home to Ireland. A lot had happened to me since the 24th of September, the day I arrived in America. For one thing my long hair was shorn and I now sported an American crew cut. I had developed as an athlete and had beaten some of the finest runners in the world. As a person I was more confident and showed the signs of my American education. On arrival home I was to discover, too, that I had developed an American accent. This was not appreciated by the locals, who looked on me as a sort of returned Yank. My mother nearly threw me out of the house when she saw the crew cut. 'My God, what have you done to your head?' she said, and after closer inspection, 'What'll the neighbours think?'

After a few weeks home in Dublin my hair grew and I lost my American accent and gradually I was reinstated with family and friends. I ran a few races, too, and had some epic struggles with an old opponent, Derek Johnson, England's silver-medalist-to-be in the Melbourne Olympics. In the process I lowered the Irish half-mile record to 1:50 on grass, a personal best. But, most significantly, I started on the road to a Melbourne crown when I ran my first compet-

Ahead of Derek Johnson (Britain) on the 2nd bend in a half-mile race in College Park, June 1955. I finished second.

itive mile in Dublin in early August. Jumbo Elliott had always insisted I would be a miler but until then no one had prevailed upon me to compete in the longer distance. Basically I was lazy, I suppose, and did not relish the prospect of running four laps instead of two. It took the combined guile and persuasion of Billy Morton and my father to convince me to have a go. Happily for me and my future in athletics, the experiment was a success. I ran and won in a new Irish record of 4:05.8, a respectable time in those days.

After a wonderful busman's holiday, I returned once more in September to Villanova's campus to continue with my studies and my track career. Coach Elliott welcomed me back and immediately enthused over my mile performance in Dublin. From now on, he informed me, I was to eat, drink and sleep the mile, with the Melbourne Olympic 1,500-metre title as our objective. In retrospect, I can admire his foresight, judgment, faith and confidence in me, although at the time I was not so sure I was going to enjoy this new and more exhausting distance. For anyone with an abundance of stamina and adequate speed the half mile is a snip. Not so the mile. Those extra two laps have the facility to sap every last ounce of energy out of a tired body, as I was soon to find out. Somehow the magic of the mile has fired the imagination of the sporting public over the years. Equally so, the mile has succeeded better than any other race in separating the men from the boys in track and field.

But lighter moments were ahead in that fall of '55. I began to go out with some of the local colleens and naturally fell victim to their many charms. I discovered, too, that the American coeds were not averse to bringing you home to meet Mum and Dad and all the family. Usually Mum took one look at my gaunt six-foot frame, all 146 pounds of me, and decided I needed some fattening up, else I would fade off the earth entirely. I would have made a good advertisement for a CARE package and the American mother out of the kindness of her heart fed me to the gills. Thanks be to God, too, for at this stage I was beginning to grumble like the rest in Villanova at the institutional cooking served up in the cafeteria. I must admit, though, that my grumbling was more part of an act to be one of the boys rather than honest complaint.

As a sophomore I was eligible to run on the varsity cross-country

With Don Bowden (University of California) the first American 4-minute miler at our training camp, Santa Cruz, California, 1960.

team. This was fun, for there was real team spirit among the harriers. Such squad runners as John Kopil, George Browne and Bill Rock who never quite made the big time in individual races were the backbone of the cross-country team. Alex Breckenridge and I ran one-two throughout the season and led Villanova to an unbeaten record for the first time in twenty-five years. Then, in early December, the board track was laid down out of doors. It was a rickety old contraption at the best of times, with the added disadvantage of 12 laps to the mile instead of the usual 11. But Jumbo rightly claimed that after you learned to master the Villanova boards it was like running out of doors when you hit the larger 11-lap tracks of the Boston and New York Gardens and elsewhere.

Our first meet was scheduled for mid-January in the K of C Games in Boston. Jumbo's plan was to run me in a few 1,000-yard cup races early in the season, moving me up to the mile later on. But this was to be changed. A series of events were to culminate in my running the mile, and only the mile, all season. Throughout December I trained exclusively with the 1,000-yard race in view. Our preparation was so intensive that I was unable to take a holiday job over Christmas. Kay Elliott, Jumbo's charming wife, entertained Breckenridge and me during the holiday period in her home. We enjoyed a real American family Christmas, participating in the trimming of the tree, exchanging gifts and all. Immediately after Christmas I damaged all my toes by wearing too tight a pair of shoes on a road run. The toes became septic and I was rushed down to the clinic of Dr John Healey, a good Irishman, for examination. This very beautiful nurse stuck all sorts of needles in me in her quest to ascertain how badly infected my toes were. Despite her beauty there was something callous about the way she prodded me, prompting me to inform her that she was the most bloodthirsty creature I had ever set eyes upon. She obviously enjoyed her work. The outcome of all the tests was that I had to undergo minor surgery on two toes and terminate training for at least two weeks. This was a tremendous disappointment to me and I felt, at the time, that it had put an end to my hopes for a successful indoor campaign.

Fortunately I healed up faster than anticipated and one week prior to the Boston games I recommenced training. My layoff had no ill effects and Coach Elliott decided to enter me in the 1,000 yards as planned. Wes Santee, the greatest mile attraction in America at that time, was down to run in the mile at the same meet. He, too, was experiencing fitness problems and at the eleventh hour withdrew, leaving the featured mile event without its Hamlet. The meet promoter, Ding Dussault, asked Jumbo to have me step into the breach. After consultation and a heavy dose of the inimitable Elliott psychology, I was persuaded and found myself lining up at the start of the O'Reilly Mile. It was a pedestrian affair and I ran home an easy winner by five yards over Len Truex in 4:11.2. Little did I know then that this was the first in a series of 34 straight mile victories I was to enjoy on the boards over the next four years. Some of these races would be just as slow as the first one, to the disgust particularly of New York fans, and some would be won in new world-record figures. Many others would not be won so easily, a foot or inches at times spelling the difference between victory and defeat for me. And in maintaining this unbeaten streak I had to shoulder the extra burden of a tremendous psychological weight, particularly as the years and number of victories mounted up. I was to be the target for every miler around. If I had realised the mental and physical strain I was to undergo, in addition to the boos and catcalls of the New York crowd, I might have quit right there and then.

Santee continued to remain on the injured list and withdrew from the mile in the *Philadelphia Inquirer* Games, my next meet. This was possibly fortunate for me, for I might not have been ready to meet and defeat a fit Santee. It was a real year for cripples. Fred Dwyer, No. 2 on the American list of milers, was injured also. It looked as though I was going to have the mile all to myself throughout the indoor season. Without Santee or Dwyer in the race, I ran a winning 4:16.9 mile in the *Inquirer* Games. It was so slow we were nearly tripping over one another and the race only came to life in the final two laps. Then there was a mad charge for the finishing line, which was reasonably exciting for us, the

Delany Booed, Tells Town He Won't Run Faster

By MILTON RICHMAN

NEW YORK (UPI)—Angry Ron Delany told the "New York crowds" to like it or lump it—he isn't going to run any faster than necessary.

Turns out Delany has a touch of Ted Williams in him. He doesn't appreciate being booed when he is, like last Saturday night at Madison Square Garden, he's apt to tell off his detractors.

The skinny mile kingpin from Dublin complained rather bitterly about "the New York crowds which always boo me" after he had dropped down from his mile specialty to win the half-mile event in the relatively slow time of 1:52.2.

Delany said he didn't get that kind of treatment anywhere else. The victory was his 34th straight indoors and it made less of an impression with the crowd than the band which blared away in the Garden stands.

Cheer John Thomas

The record-hungry crowd, however, gave an ear-piercing ovation to 17-year-old John Thomas of Boston University, who high jumped seven feet for the second time in as many meets.

"I definitely think I will do better," said Thomas.

He'll get his chance next Saturday in the 71st national championships at the Garden, the same meet in which Delany will return to competition in the mile event and shoot for his 35th straight triumph indoors.

Delany barely beat Manhattan's Tom Murphy to the tape in running his first half-mile event in

five years. Former Pitt star Arnie Sowell, who holds the world record of 1:50.3, was third and Mike Rawson of Britain fourth.

Delany discovered he couldn't run his own race so much in the half-mile as he ordinarily does in the mile.

"In the mile," he said, "I can gamble and lay back. But in the half-mile I have to stay up with the leaders."

Thomas was all alone in his brilliant leap, a jump that proved to be the highlight of the New York Athletic Club meet. Three competitors who wound up in a tie for second place could clear only six feet, five inches.

Beats Europeans

With Delany out of the mile, Phil Coleman, the American steeplechase champion from Chicago, captured that event in 4:08.6. In winning, Coleman beat two of Europe's celebrated sub-four minute milers, Laszlo Tabori of Hungary and Brian Hewson of Britain.

Mel Barnwell of the University of Pittsburgh equalled the world indoor record of 6.1 in winning the 60-yard dash, but pole-vaulter Don Bragg, who set a world indoor record of 15 feet, 9¼ inches in Philadelphia on Friday, won his event with a routine 15 foot, 4½ inch effort.

Bill Dellinger of Oregon was far off his 8:50 record in winning the two-mile event with a clocking of 8:59.8, and in other events, Josh Culbreath of the Philadelphia Pioneer Club won the 500 yard run in 57.7, while Elias Gilbert of Winston Salem Teachers took the 60-yard high hurdles in 7.3.

INQUIRER

15th Annual Philadelphia

GAMES

February 13th 1959 Convention Hall

SOUVENIR PROGRAM 50¢

SPONSORED BY THE PHILADELPHIA INQUIRER CHARITIES, INC.

competitors, but probably an utter bore to the spectators.

I was not displeased with my perfomance, for I always had a strict run-to-win attitude. Record chasing was not my game. My psychological makeup would not allow me to push myself against the clock. This hesitancy to run solely against time expressed itself even in my training sessions. The most dreaded words Jumbo could utter were, 'Ron, I want you to do a time trial today.' I hated and detested them. I needed the competitive urgency of someone breathing down my neck or running alongside or in front of me to spur me on. The idea of running against a stopwatch for the glory of some sort of record or other did not register with me. I loved to compete man against man and may the best man win. This attitude of mine was never to please the record-crazy public. The crowd wanted me to run for records. But I could never quite figure out where it would all end if I succumbed to their urgings. The spectator doesn't use his reason. If an athlete breaks the record one weekend, they expect him to do even better on his next outing. They are never satisfied.

Wes Santee was ready to run the mile in the BAA Games in Boston, where the previous year he had set a world record of 4:03.8 for the distance. And I was ready to take him on, world record or no world record. I hadn't beaten 4:11 indoors yet in my previous two victories, but I was confident I could run much faster. Santee was America's hope then for a four-minute mile and was a flamboyant and colourful character. He was a real prima donna and played the part to perfection. Wes usually brought his own pacemaker with him wherever he raced. The BAA Games were no exception. Bill Taylor, a runner I had never heard of, a Marine buddy of Santee's, was entered for the sole purpose of ensuring a hot pace in the early stages of the competition.

It was a fantastic race. Taylor hit the front at the off with Santee on his heels. I settled in at the back of the field with Bill Tidwell for company. It was a scorcher. Taylor and Santee ran 58.6 seconds for the first quarter mile, sensationally fast time in those days. Taylor continued to pile on the pressure, leading Santee through the half mile in two minutes flat before dropping out of the race. Meanwhile, about 60 yards behind the leaders, I was engaged in an elbows match with Tidwell. For some reason or other Billy began thumping me in the back. I remember swinging an arm back at Billy and then suddenly waking up and realising I was 60 yards behind Santee with only five laps to go. Immediately I snapped into gear for the first time in the race. I began pulling back the yards on Santee. He was timed at 3:03.6 at the three-quarters but was tiring badly. There was still a gap of 3 yards between us, but I drew on my reserves of strength and with a lap to go passed him and went on to win in 4:06.3 In the process I ran my last quarter in 57 seconds.

It was a great thrill beating the American champion. I was very flattered when after the race Wes said that he considered me a threat even to John Landy for the 1,500-metre title at Melbourne, though I suspected his judgment at the time, especially since he had run against me only on the one occasion.

I was looking forward to my mile duels with Santee for the rest of the season when the AAU stepped in and suspended him, pending an investigation that he had been paid exorbitant expenses for his previous appearances at American meets. The outcome of this investigation was to be the untimely banning of Santee for life from competing in amateur athletics. I am sure if Wes had not impaired his amateur status he would have contributed substantially to the history of the mile and would have undoubtedly been America's first four-minute miler.

With Santee out of the way I had no difficulty in running out the indoor season undefeated, eight run, eight won. I had more difficulty with the spectators than my opponents. I first got the hoots in Philadelphia following my 4:16-plus effort but I did not mind, for after all Philadelphia was my 'home town' by adoption. But the New York rail birds let me have it with a vengeance following my victory in the AAU mile in 4:14.5, a schoolboyish time in their estimation. I was hooted and jeered at for running so slow by some of the fattest slobs I have ever seen. I was amused, for I could not help thinking that these same boyos could hardly walk, never mind run. By the time the K of C meet came around, the last race of the season in New York, thank God, I was even being pelted with paper cups thrown from the gallery during the race. I was grateful the beer was not sold in cans. Another disgruntled fan threw a penny at me, the cheapskate. Perhaps his intention was to insult me, not hit me. Seriously, though, I did not like being booed one bit. I tried to treat it as dispassionately as possible but often felt like giving the fans the Ted Williams treatment. When questioned by the press I always maintained that the jeers did not upset me. I expounded to them on my 'run to win only' philosophy. Inside I was burning mad, but what could I do? I could not take on 15,000 people all at once out in the alley. Instead I was outwardly passive and unmoved and showed no emotion when getting the razz. Similarly, when I eventually won the respect of the New York track fans with world records, exciting doubles and down-to-wire victories, I could never warm to their applause. I could never help feeling that next week I would be getting that old familiar treatment.

I heaved a big sigh of relief when the indoor season ended. I looked forward to a few weeks' rest before heading into the outdoor season and ultimately a date in November at the Melbourne Olympics. The Games were now only eight months away and I could look back on the indoor season with satisfaction. My series of victories had helped my confidence considerably. My buildup was going as planned. But I was to suffer a few shocks in the next few months: defeats, a near crippling injury and, worse still, doubts regarding my selection by Ireland to compete in the Games at all.

First, the defeats. On Saturday afternoon, May 5, I took on John Landy of Australia in one of the most publicised mile races of the century at the Coliseum in Los Angeles. This was to be a dress rehearsal for the Olympics as far as I was concerned. Discarding my usual tactic of staying back off the pace, I bolted into the lead at the start of the race. Within half a lap I was 20 yards up on Landy but going far too fast. In my inexperience I had run the first furlong in a flying 26 seconds. The quarter time was under 57 seconds, a killing pace, and I was still out in front by some 15 yards. By the halfway mark I began to tie up and was passed shortly afterward by Landy and Jim Bailey, another Australian. I struggled home in 4:05, with Bailey handing Landy a shock defeat in a sub-four-minute clocking for both.

If I hadn't run too smartly, I at least spent my time off the track wisely listening to Landy's advice on how to run the mile. John pointed out flaws in my action, which I worked on subsequently, and he assured me it was only a matter of time before I, too, would join the Four Minute Club.

Vanquished though I was, my Villanova classmates did not desert me. When I arrived home a party of 300 met me at the airport and cheered me as though I had won. It was as if they were saying, 'We have faith in you, Ronnie. Don't quit now.' Also, in my absence they had elected me treasurer of my class. It was remarked that I was the first Villanovan to use television in my campaign, a reference to the nationally televised Landy race.

On one of my nightly visits to the Villanova Library to study.

A week later I again saw the green-vested back of Landy running another sub-four-minute mile in the Fresno Relays, while I followed him home some 75 yards behind. This form did not exactly augur too well for my Olympic hopes. I had hardly time to lick my wounds, for immediately on my return to Villanova I had to sit exams. This was probably the best thing that could have happened, for my mind was taken off track completely and I did not have time to be depressed or disappointed. Exams were no particular bother to me. My approach to studies was the same as it was to athletics. I never studied particularly hard but studied regularly. I established a pattern of going over to the library each evening after dinner and staying there until closing time. Many nights I would fall asleep at the study table from the sheer exhaustion of a hard training session. One of the librarians would usually awaken me when it was time to go home. With the strict silence rule in the library I could really get a good sleep. This, of course, was not my reason for going there. I had the honest intention of studying, but when fatigue set in my head would droop and I would doze off. Another attraction of the library was the chance of meeting some talent from the local girls' colleges. A real stir would move through the reading room as soon as some strange female came in the door. All eyes, except those of the very dedicated, would turn and follow her movements step by step to where she would choose to sit. If she was pretty, or, more important, well built, very little study would be done from then on. Instead, the lads would find some reason to consult the books on the shelves nearest to her, at the same time getting a closer look at the merchandise. When the young lady got up to leave, half the boys would trail out after her. Now that I think of it, I must have missed seeing a lot of talent while I slept.

Inset: *Getting the better of Lang Stanley in a half-mile race, Stockton, California, 2 June 1956.*

Main: *Ron and Don by the sea: sand dune training on the Pacific coast, March, 1960.*

OLYMPIC ODYSSEY

ULTIMATE TRIUMPH: THE OLYMPIC 1,500

First printed in *Sports Illustrated*, January 29, 1968

The years of learning, of training, of agony and ecstasy came to a glorious peak at the Melbourne Games when Delany swept to victory.

After completing exams the Villanova track team headed west in May of 1956 to compete in the Compton Invitational meet and the National Collegiate Championships. The American boys on our squad had a lot at stake for they were trying to make the final tryouts for the Melbourne Olympics. Charlie Jenkins and Phil Reavis were to be successful and gain selection on the American team. As an Irishman

1956 Olympic Team Visit, Áras an Uachtaráin, 29 December 1956. Pictured with President Seán T. O'Ceallaigh and Bean O'Ceallaigh.

I was under considerably less pressure. We have no tryouts in Ireland. An Irish Olympic Council sets standards for the various events, and if an athlete meets the required standard he is eligible for selection. For my own part I had already bettered the standards set for the half mile and the mile, 1:50 and 4:05.8 respectively. But I still did not know if I would be selected and was not to know officially for a long time yet.

At that time Irish sport was very complex at the organisational level. In our small country we had three different athletic bodies administering the sport of track and field. For various reasons, political and otherwise, they did not see eye to eye. As a result, the Irish Olympic Council, which is made up of representatives of the various Olympic sports such as boxing, fencing and weightlifting, did not have any representative of track and field on its board. This amounted to our athletics team being selected by persons with no knowledge of or connection with the sport. This misfortunate system almost led to my not going to Melbourne.

But, for now, back to Compton. After my defeats by John Landy I

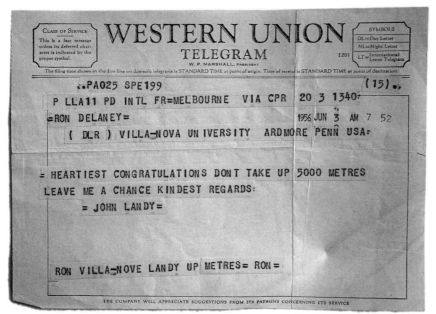

A nice telegram from John Landy congratulating me on running my first 4-minute mile. In the previous month John had easily beaten me in LA and Fresno, California.

was paradoxically not nearly as anxious about my miling and my desire to beat four minutes. I was in a relaxed frame of mind, and I was not thinking specifically of trying to break through the magic barrier. There was a classy field lined up for the Compton Mile. World 1,500-metre record holder Gunnar Nielsen of Denmark headed the list. The American challenge included Fred Dwyer, formerly of Villanova, and Bobby Seaman, a rising UCLA star. Before the race I was more concerned with getting a pair of spikes to run in, for my old ones were worn out, than in preparing myself for the race. I got a pair on credit about 15 minutes before the off from a shoe salesman at the meet. He made me pay up afterward, too, my last $10 in fact, in spite of the exciting result of the race. He obviously didn't appreciate the value of good public relations.

As usual, by now, there was a rabbit in the Compton Mile to ensure a fast pace. Danny Schweikart, a no more than average miler, did the early running. I lay back in the field but at no time lost contact with the leaders. Jumbo determined the 'contact point' as anywhere within ten yards of the pacesetter. I was always supposed to keep within this range. However, I must have given Jumbo many a start, for I seldom if ever could keep up early on in a race. I often felt more tired during the second lap than at any other stage, and I had this terrible tendency to dawdle along behind – completely out of touch. But in Compton I was not taking any chances and for once followed Jumbo's orders. The early part of the race, up to the three-quarter mark, was unexciting. The lead interchanged a few times between Nielsen, Dwyer and Seaman. I did not hear the three-quarter time called out, so I had no idea how fast we were going or, more important, that we were on schedule for a four-minute mile.

The final lap was a scorcher. Nielsen was being chased by Dwyer and Seaman. About 200 yards from home I began to move up. I slipped past the two Americans and into an attacking position about one yard behind the big Dane. I was only conscious that I was racing another man at this point, and I had absolutely no idea of how fast we were going. About 100 yards from the finish I moved up on Nielsen's shoulder. He was still very strong and held me off. But I was determined to pass him, for I was still smarting from the two Landy defeats. Forty yards from the tape I edged in front. I stayed there,

Left: *Finish of the Compton Mile, 1 June 1956.*

Below: *With Gunnar Nielsen (Denmark) after our first 4-minute mile.*

barely holding off Nielsen's challenge. Immediately I finished I was swarmed on by my teammates and some of the spectators. I knew I had achieved something in beating Nielsen, but I could not quite understand all this excitement. In the jumble of voices around me I thought I heard someone say I had broken the barrier. Just then over the public-address system came the voice of the announcer. There was a silence, startling in its suddenness, as he called the result of the mile and the time: 3 minutes 59 seconds.

I had made it, and Nielsen also with 3:59.1. I could hardly believe my ears. I was amazed, dumfounded. I knew I would break four minutes someday but not so soon. But, suddenly, I was the seventh four-minute miler in history. I had joined Roger Bannister, John Landy, Laszlo Tabori, Chris Chataway, Brian Hewson and Jim Bailey in the most exclusive club in the world. And, with Tabori, I was the fourth fastest miler of all time. I was full of gratitude in my heart to everyone who had helped me achieve this, and especially to Jumbo Elliott for his unceasing confidence in me.

Nielsen and I, in breaking the barrier, ended a lot of drivel at that time about the psychological aspects of four-minute miling. There was no resolution here on either side, no great tactical planning for our achievement. Rather, two men pitted against each other had run as fast as they could in an effort to defeat the other and in the process had run four minutes. Perhaps Bannister had to fight a psychological barrier to become the first to crash through, but from now on four-minute miles would become a matter of physical condition and the necessary effort required. The die had been cast.

To add to my joy, two weeks later in Berkeley, Calif. I won the NCAA 1,500-metre championship, beating Landy's recent conqueror, Jim Bailey of Oregon, in the process. So I was able to set off on the journey home to Ireland for my summer vacation happy in the knowledge that I had run a four-minute mile and had beaten Bailey. I was becoming optimistic about my chances in Melbourne – if I ever got there. But on arrival home in Dublin I discovered the members of the Irish Olympic Council had not yet made up their minds about sending me to the Olympics. Under tremendous pressure from the press and athletic officials the council met again. But they were not going to be rushed. The outcome of their meeting was a bald statement to the effect that

Ireland would be represented in Melbourne if funds were available. They mentioned certain sports, athletics included, but did not nominate any one athlete. This was most upsetting at the time and the strain of not knowing officially if I would be travelling to the Games had an adverse effect on my training. I began to wonder seriously what I would have to do to earn selection.

To add to my worries I was seriously spiked in the heel during an 800-metre race in Paris in early July. For some strange reason or other the organisers had about twenty athletes entered in the race, and they elected to start us on a turn. There was a mad stampede at the start. An Iranian athlete running his first international race ever chose, in his excitement, to try to run over me rather than around me. In the process he nearly cut my right heel off. I was taken to the hospital with two deep gashes in the heel, but the doctors said they would mend in about a month. I was greatly relieved. My relief nearly turned to horror when I saw a nurse preparing the largest injection I have ever seen in my life. I knew it was for me, but I didn't expect her to want to put it directly into my back above the shoulder blade. I tried to reason with her in my best school French, suggesting an alternative area with a little more flesh in preponderance. However, she kept insisting 'ici' and pointing to my back, so I had to succumb. I really was beginning to hate nurses. But it's an ill wind that does not blow somebody good, for after leaving the hospital, in the company of Louis Vandendries, a Belgian resident in Dublin and secretary of the Irish Amateur Athletic Union, I hobbled around the famous night spots of Paris. Knowing I was out of training for at least a month, I had a great night smoking cigars and sampling the *vin*. I had started out the evening hobbling, but I had developed a distinct roll by the time I got back to our hotel.

A month later I was back in training. After six days I ran my first race, a moderate 4:06.4 mile at London's famous White City. I then attempted the ridiculous and took on Brian Hewson of Britain, another four-minute miler, before a partisan home crowd in Dublin two days later. The result was disastrous. I finished 75 yards behind him in 4:20, the slowest mile I ever ran in my life. I learned my lesson and decided no more racing for the remainder of the summer, for obviously my layoff and injury had affected me more than I thought.

I continued to do light training, and on my return to Villanova in September, two months before the Games opened, I was moderately fit. Jumbo Elliott appreciated that my poor miles in Dublin were a result of the injury in Paris. He still believed that even with two months' training we could win the 1,500 metres in Melbourne. At this stage, believe it or not, I still did not know if I was going to be selected for the Irish team. The Irish Olympic Council had not issued any further statement since June and to date had not selected a team. This was utterly ridiculous. It meant that the aspiring Olympic hopefuls, including myself, were training in the hope and belief we would be selected, but nothing more. It was a tremendous worry. I mention this to highlight the different approaches of the small country and a track power like the US. Whereas Ireland's team was still unannounced, the US team had been selected at the final Olympic tryouts the previous June, and the team would gather shortly on the West Coast for collective training prior to going down to Australia well before the Games would open. I would arrive in Australia, as it turned out, only three days before the opening ceremonies – a very brief period in which to become acclimatised.

At Villanova that fall I trained as I had never done before, while at the same time carrying a full schedule of lectures. It meant I had to live the life of a recluse, for my training program called for two workouts a day. There was no time for dates or any sort of social life. Even movies were out. It was train, train, train, with eating, studying and sleeping fitting into the daily pattern in that order. There was one good side effect. In view of my heavy training program I was put on the training table for all meals with the football squad. The big 200-pound-plus linemen could hardly believe that such a skinny little Irishman could put so much away at table. I took quite a ribbing, all of it good humoured – not that it would have made much difference, for I was not inclined to engage in fisticuffs with any of those ballplayers, even the littlest of them.

Finally, in October, I learned from a newspaper report that I had been named to the Irish team for Melbourne. I did not get any official communication, letter or otherwise, from the council until the day before I left New York on the first leg of the long trip down under. But my mind was eased. I knew I was now going to the Games, and I was

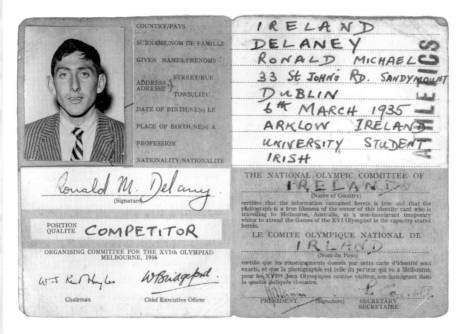

My official ID, Melbourne 1956.

even more determined than ever to win. My workouts under Coach Elliott's ever watchful eyes were progressing most satisfactorily. By the end of October I was performing better in training than ever before. I had the assistance and encouragement of all my teammates during my training sessions. Johnny Kopil and Alex Breckenridge, no mean milers themselves, were particularly helpful. In my more strenuous workouts they would each run an alternate lap with me, pushing me to the limit of my endurance. All the time Jumbo was drumming into my brain his particular philosophy on running to win. 'There is only one place to finish,' he would say, 'first. The rest are nobodies. It is not sufficient to run well, better than you have ever run before, Ron, and perhaps take a place. If you want the glory, if you want to go down in history, you must win.'

I knew Jumbo believed in me. This, above all, gave me great confidence. His attitude regarding winning really sunk home. He had me worked up to such a pitch that nothing else was going to satisfy me. I wanted to win and I would win, for him, my country and myself. Jumbo, my teammates and my father were probably the only ones who gave me more than a snowball's chance in hell. The press had written me off because of my poor showing in Dublin the previous August. In their opinion Landy was the favourite, with the other members of the four-minute club, Bailey, Hewson, Tabori and Nielsen, tipped to fill the minor placings. Rozsavolgyi, the Hungarian who was now the 1,500-metre world-record holder, was also listed among the favourites. But I was not concerned. I knew I was fitter than I had ever been before in my life – far fitter than when I had run my own four-minute effort the previous June. What did it matter what the press and the experts thought? I was in my most positive frame of mind ever as a result of Jumbo's buildup. Nothing had been neglected. My body and mind were conditioned as never before – to strain to breaking point, if necessary, for victory. Still without official communication from the Irish Olympic Council, I learned from the grapevine in early November what the travel arrangements for the Irish party to Australia were. I was to link up with the team in New York and travel on from there with them. They were due in New York from Dublin on the second Sunday in November. On Saturday morning I still had heard nothing from the Irish Olympic Council. My travel tickets had not yet arrived, though I knew they would. Nothing was going to prevent me from going to Australia now. The Villanova post office closed at noon on Saturday, but I arranged with the postmaster to let me come back to check again in mid-afternoon. When I did, a special-delivery letter awaited me. It was from the secretary of the Irish Olympic Council and he enclosed the air tickets, full instructions regarding the trip and sundry identity cards and documents. Better late than never, I thought, but certainly not in the best interest of an athlete trying to prepare for competition.

The next day I travelled to New York and checked in for my flight to San Francisco, where the Irish team would train for a few days before continuing on to Australia. The flight I was to take had originated in Shannon, and the Irish team was on board. I met my teammates for the first time in the tourist-class cabin of that old Super Constellation. They were a grand bunch of lads, with one girl, Maeve Kyle, included. Altogether, our Irish Olympians numbered twelve – one yachtsman, three athletes, seven boxers and a wrestler. Yet among us we were to bring home to Ireland one gold, one silver and three bronze medals, on average the best performance of any country in the Games. We stopped off in San Francisco and worked out in Berkeley at the University of California. Brutus Hamilton, the university's track coach and one of the finest gentlemen I have ever met, helped me with my workouts. At the end of the week, following my final session under his care, he told me there was just one other thing we had to do. He instructed me to go down the track about 20 yards from the finishing line. He then pulled out a piece of finishing tape from his pocket, attached it to the post, stretched it out over the track and said, 'Come on, run through it.' I obeyed and amid our laughter Mr Hamilton explained that he believed an athlete should practise everything, even breaking the tape. I was then fully prepared for Melbourne.

We left San Francisco on November 17, only five days before the

Stopover in Fiji on the way to Melbourne, 18 November 1956 (l-r) Eamon Kinsella, Maeve Kyle, Ronnie Delany and Gerry Martina (wrestling).

Games were to open, and headed down for Melbourne via Honolulu, Fiji and Sydney. In the early evening of November 19 we arrived in the Olympic city to a tumultuous welcome from a myriad of Irish-Australian societies, with Irish pipers and colleens, dressed in national costume, on hand for the occasion. The Irish down under were thrilled to see their old country represented in the Games and extended to us the heartiest of good luck and best wishes. We arrived at the Olympic Village and settled in immediately, tired and needing to rest up after our long journey. But before going to bed we raised an Irish flag outside our quarters. As it so happened, it was the largest flag put up – the other nations had standard-sized ones – and before we knew it every newspaperman in the village was outside photographing it. It caused a sensation. Next morning matters were put right – or wrong, depending on which way you look at it – when the camp commandant came along with the proper-sized flag, took our big one down and went through a formal ceremony of unfurling the new flag.

My first days in the village were filled with meeting members of other nations' teams with whom I was acquainted. It was great seeing my teammates from Villanova, Charlie Jenkins and Phil Reavis, both competing, of course, for the US. Charlie had a store of information on my opponents; he had done some research for me. He told me Landy was having trouble with his legs and Bailey trouble with his nose and that the one-two threat of the Australians was considered weakened. Rozsavolgyi and Tabori of Hungary and the British team of Hewson, Wood and Boyd were all thought highly of by the experts. The tension in the village itself was electric. All about me were lean, strained faces with eyes sunk deep from the rigour of long hours of training. Everywhere there was talk of who would win this and that, all of which, if you listened to it, would only make you twice as

Top: Stopover in Honolulu on the way back from Australia, with John Ford (director of The Quiet Man) *and Lord Killanin.*

Above: Team members with the Columban Fathers in Melbourne (l-r) Eamon Kinsella, Fred Tiedt (silver medallist), Gerry Martina and Harry Perry.

nervous and tense. For the most part I kept to myself and my Irish teammates. Shortly after my arrival in the village I met the three Britons, Hewson, Wood and Boyd. Despite our centuries of differences we Irish and British were friendly toward one another. They were all talk about who was going to win the 1,500 metres and mentioned everyone's name, practically. I gathered they were in a state of high tension and when they asked me who I thought would win I announced blandly, 'Myself.' I might as well have insulted the Queen, it had such an effect on them. One of them actually screamed. The last thing they wanted to hear apparently was one of their competitors saying he was going to win. Admittedly, I said it more out of bravado than in belief I could do it. But in cold-war terms the Irish had put one over on the British again.

On November 22 the opening ceremony of the XVI Olympiad took place. Sixty-seven nations' contingents of athletes paraded into Olympic Stadium before a capacity crowd exceeding 100,000. Even if one were never to win an Olympic medal, the memory of the opening ceremony would last a lifetime in one's mind, I believe. Somehow every athlete I have spoken to on the subject has expressed the same sentiment. There is something very special, historic and significant in being sent by your country to an Olympic Games, and this realisation comes to you as you participate in the opening ceremony before the eyes of the world. The taking of the Olympic oath, the fanfares of trumpets, the choirs, the lighting of the Olympic flame, the releasing of the doves of peace carrying their message that the Games are on – all combine to make a great spectacle and an undying impression on the mind of the participants. I was proud of my heritage and my native land as I stood erect in the Olympic Stadium, a privileged member of the Irish team.

I was not due to run until a week later in the preliminary heats of the 1,500 metres. I did not go to the track and field events for more than an hour each day. I found the tension too great. I had the thrill of seeing Charlie Jenkins win the 400-metre crown and believe I could have won the high jump with my exultant leap as he breasted the tape. The days flew by and I was preparing myself mentally for the task ahead. I reasoned I was as fit and strong as anyone in the race. I was faster than most over a half mile or quarter and a four-minute miler to boot. I believed I had it in me to win. I was almost alone in this opinion, except for my coach, my family and my closest friends. No one looked for the reason for my defeats; the fact that I was spiked in Paris and out of training for three weeks was completely ignored. In retrospect, it is probably a good thing not to be favoured.

Left: Charles Jenkins (USA) on the victory podium after his 400-metre win, with silver medallist Karl Haas (Germany) and bronze medallists Hellsten (Finland) and Ignatyev (Russia).

The heats of the 1,500 metres were held on Thursday, but qualifying for the final turned out to be a mere formality. The first four in each of the three heats went on to the final on Saturday. I strolled home in third place in my heat comfortably behind Merv Lincoln of Australia and Ken Wood of Great Britain, with the much favoured Tabori of Hungary in the fourth spot. The other qualifiers were Landy, Nielsen, Hewson, Ian Boyd, Klaus Richtzenhain, Neville Scott, Murray Halberg and Stanislav Jungwirth. Rozsavolgyi, the world record holder, was eliminated along with Joseph Barthel, the defending Olympic champion; Dan Waern, the greatest Swedish runner since Gunder Hagg; the Germans,

THE OLYMPIC GAMES MELBOURNE 1956

Gunther Dohrow and Siegfried Herrmann; and all three American contestants. Jim Bailey of Australia scratched from his heat.

The final was wide open despite Landy's position as favourite. There were four other four-minute milers in the field beside myself – Landy, Hewson, Tabori and Nielsen – and I was younger than any of them. Halberg and Scott of New Zealand were comparatively inexperienced. Lincoln of Australia had probably run too fast in winning his heat. Richtzenhain of Germany and Jungwirth of Czechoslovakia were unknown quantities. Of the two other Britons in the race, Wood was considered a dark horse, but Boyd hardly seemed up to the class of the race.

Friday was spent resting and relaxing as far as possible under the trying circumstances. Every moment my mind was turning over analysing my opponents. It was virtually impossible to decide on the form of the field. Finally I settled to my own satisfaction that Landy was still my greatest threat, with Hewson the next most likely to succeed in beating me to my life's ambition. I also considered the possibility of an outsider of the inspired sort who suddenly appears in Olympic finals and performs way above himself, running off with the laurels. It was this sort of inspiration I was hoping for myself.

The day I had lived for dawned bright and warm. It was difficult to remain calm but I tried as best I could, for I knew every moment of anxiety used up valuable energy. I resigned myself quietly to the will of God and prayed not so much for victory but the grace to run up to my capabilities. When I arrived at Olympic Stadium I immediately went to the warm-up area for the 'roll call' and to prepare for my race. One of the first people I met was Charlie Jenkins and in spite of the seriousness of the occasion for me he could not restrain himself from bursting into laughter when he saw the anxiety written all over my face. I'll always remember what he said to me: 'Man, I know what you're going through. I'm sure glad my ordeal is over.' He could well laugh with his Olympic gold medal already secured and with the possibility of another before him in the 1,600-metre relay final later in the day.

Before I fully realised it, the race was called and we were marched single file through a dark tunnel out into the sudden glaring brightness of the Olympic oval before 100,000 partisan fans ready to cheer on their hero, John Landy. Yet, as we moved across the stadium toward the starting area, John came over to me and wished me good luck. It was typical of this great sportsman.

It is funny how even in life's most serious moments one cannot help being amused by some little detail: the three British athletes were moving around as if they were glued together, all ashen-faced and looking as if they were going to the gallows rather than the starting line. I remember reprimanding myself and thinking I would not be so amused if one of these Englishmen were ahead of me at the finish.

There was one false start; we were lined up again; the pistol fired and the Olympic 1,500-metre final was on. In a crowded field of twelve one had to avoid trouble and I did this by running at the back of the pack. After 400 metres in 58.9, Halberg was leading, with Hewson nicely placed and a bunched field right behind. Lincoln took the lead at the 800-metre mark in 2:00.3, with his compatriot Landy last and

Below: About to pass Brian Hewson on the last bend, with Richtzenhain (Germany), Boyd (GB), Landy (Australia) and Jungwirth (Czechoslovakia) (in that order).

myself just in front of him. At the bell the entire field was fantastically gathered within a mere six yards. Lincoln, Hewson and Richtzenhain was the order of the leaders. I was back in tenth place but I was very much in touch with the leaders, for the pace at this stage of the race was not troubling me. I knew I could not afford to allow anyone to break into a lead at this vital stage of the race so I moved out wide to allow myself a clear run about 350 yards from the finish. As we went down the backstretch for the last time Hewson was forging away in the lead. Suddenly Landy sprinted and I reacted immediately, slipping into his wake and following him as we passed the struggling figures of the other competitors. I knew if I were to win I would have to make one and

only one decisive move. I restrained myself as long as possible, and about 150 yards from the finish I opened up with everything I had. Within 10 yards I was in the lead and going away from the field. I knew nobody was going to pass me, for my legs were pumping like pistons, tired but not going to give in to anybody. My heart swelled with joy as I approached the tape 10 feet clear of the rest of the field,

Top: Breasting the tape, followed by Richtzenhain, Landy and Hewson.

Above: John Landy helps me to my feet after my moment of prayer.

and as I burst through I threw my arms wide in exultation. I could hardly believe I had won. My eyes swelled with tears, and I dropped to my knees in a prayer of thanksgiving. John Landy, who finished third, came over to me, helped me to my feet and warmly congratulated me. The Australian crowd was showing its

sportsmanship by generously applauding me.

It was the happiest day of my life. I had set out to win the Olympic 1,500-metre crown, and with the help of Jumbo Elliott I had achieved my goal. The rest of my athletic career would always be a sort of anticlimax. I was plagued by injuries later on and I never again had the same driving ambition. But on that day in Melbourne I was grateful to so many people – my parents, my early coaches in Ireland, Jumbo and John Landy – who had inspired me with confidence and example.

From now on I was an Olympic Champion. To this very day the after

Opposite page: With John Landy, Brian Hewson and Neville Scott (New Zealand) moments after my win. No 166, Murray Halberg (New Zealand), is also pictured.

Above left: Congratulating a victorious John Landy after his 4-minute mile at the West Coast relays, Fresno, California, 12 May 1956.

effects linger on. Whether it is New York, London, Paris or Dublin, I enjoy the friendship and the welcome of athletes and officials alike. I have long since retired from active participation but I find that every sports fraternity I encounter renders me respect because I am an Olympic Champion. It is as if you are a living part of history. One can break world records, as I did in my time, and they are forgotten. But when you win an Olympic title you live on as part of the sport after you retire from active competition. There are responsibilities to live up to also. I am always conscious of the need to give youth good example by word and action. I believe as an Olympic champion I should keep in good physical trim – I don't want to hear someone remark about me one day, 'See that fat slob over there? He won the Olympics way back in 1956.' And the answer, 'No, not him. You're kidding me.'

A great subject of debate in Ireland even to this day is, 'Would Delany have won the Olympics if he had not gone to Villanova?' I think I can answer that question once and for all. There is no doubt in my mind that I would not have won an Olympic title if I had remained in Ireland. I benefited and developed under the expert tuition of Jumbo Elliott. I learned tactical sense from my many skirmishes on the board tracks. And above all I competed against the best competition available week after week, year after year, throughout the US, whether it was a native son like Tom Courtney or a foreign import like John Landy.

I am eternally grateful that I was afforded the opportunity of living in America and attending Villanova University.

My education has helped me to achieve a good standard of living in my own country, and my athletic experiences are enough to fill a lifetime with memories. I have more than reaped a rich harvest for the effort I have put into track and field!

HOMECOMING 1956

The story of my homecoming to Ireland following my Olympic triumph is very special to me. *Sports Illustrated* sent along a senior reporter Gerald Holland 'to record the sights and the sounds and the words and the music and the grand affair'. I don't think I could ever have captured in my own words this magical time for me, my family and my friends. Gerald Holland did and he answered the question I have often been asked over the years – 'What was it like when you came home after the Olympics?' 'A New Irish Hero Goes Home' appeared in the 21 January issue of *Sports Illustrated* in 1957. It was accompanied by some memorable photographs by Brian Seed from London. Brian also took the contemporary photographs that appeared with my own series of articles in *Sports Illustrated* in 1968. Even to this day I feel a sense of indebtedness to Gerald and Brian who with their disparate skills recorded for posterity aspects of my life as an international sports celebrity and captured the Ireland of that time.

A NEW IRISH HERO GOES HOME

And Sports Illustrated, *searching its staff, finds a County Clare man (once-removed) to go along to Dublin with Ron Delany and share with its readers all the grand affairs welcoming the Olympic winner*
   By GERALD HOLLAND

Ronald Michael Delany, the 21-year-old Villanova University commerce and finance student who beat the best milers in the world in the Olympic 1,500 metres, flew home to Ireland for the Christmas holidays, and *Sports Illustrated* sent me along to see what kind of a hero's welcome the old country would give him.

   I told Jim Cahill, the TWA man, as we stood waiting at the check-in counter at Idlewild Airport in New York, that I had never met Ronnie, and Cahill said he hadn't either. But then we both recognised him from his pictures as he came hurrying through the crowd. Wearing a duffel coat and carrying a tweed topcoat, he looked very tall and very thin and very Irish with his black, tousled hair and his high colour and his blue eyes and his sharply angular face that became actually handsome when he smiled. And he was smiling in a minute at the girl who had just told him there would be a charge for overweight.

'Ah,' laughed Ronnie softly, 'a nice girl like you wouldn't be charging me, now would you, for a little overweight when I've flown all around the world with TWA?'

It didn't work (although the girl couldn't help smiling), and as Ronnie reached for his wallet, Jim Cahill moved over and introduced himself and then said, 'Did you know there's a writer going with you?'

'Ah, yes,' said Ronnie, making a face, 'Jumbo Elliott [his coach at Villanova] told me, and isn't it a nuisance? I'm that weary of pressmen.'

Jim Cahill leaned over and whispered, 'He's right behind you.'

'Oh, oh,' exclaimed Ronnie, drawing his coat collar up in embarrassment. Then he turned quickly around with his winning smile and put out his hand.

'I'm very glad to meet you,' he said, 'and I'm just sorry I'm the cause of taking you away from home at Christmas time.'

I waited until we were well out over the sea to tell Ronnie that I had no intention of interviewing him in a pressman's usual way, but was simply going along to observe the celebration. Then, in an offhand way, I confided that I myself was the son of a County Clare man.

Soon we were talking away at a great rate (I was getting more Irish by the minute), and Ronnie was reaching up in the luggage rack and taking down a toy kangaroo he had brought from Australia for his girl friend and childhood sweetheart, Elisabeth MacArthur. Before we knew it, we were over Shannon Airport, two and a half hours ahead of schedule, thanks to a solid tailwind.

Right: Welcomed home by family and friends at Shannon Airport, 4 a.m., 19 December 1956.

'That's too bad altogether,' said Ronnie. 'If we were on schedule I'd expect my father to meet me. But at half three in the morning, nobody will be here. I suggest we go to a hotel in Limerick and sleep a few hours.'

A few minutes later an astounded Ronnie Delany found himself in the midst of a wildly cheering crowd of several hundred that included not only his father but his mother and his brothers Joe and Paddy and his sister Colette, and pretty Elisabeth MacArthur herself. There were a dozen pressmen from the Dublin newspapers and

*Left: With Mum
and Dad on my
arrival home to
Shannon Airport,
early
in the morning,
19 December 1956.*

photographers and a rather tense press conference (Sample question: 'Will you continue to run?' Sample answer: 'Well, I'm twenty-one years old. What do you want me to do – retire?'). Lord Killanin, the president of the Irish Olympic Council, was there and Captain Theo Ryan, the

president of the Crusaders, Ronnie's athletic club, and stocky, grey-haired Billy Morton, Dublin's promoter of amateur track events and the man who first proposed that Ronnie try running the mile.

Thus began a day that was one happy blur, with a breakfast at Hotel Glentworth in Limerick, an official reception by the mayor of Limerick at the Town Hall, and then the triumphal motorcade from Limerick to Dublin, with scheduled stops for official welcoming ceremonies and quite a few unscheduled stops like the poignantly vivid one pictured above. This was 63 miles from Dublin. On a hillside, around a turning in the road, stood a line of boys, ten to twelve perhaps, the tin-whistle band of De La Salle School of the Christian Brothers. One of the young Brothers was acting as conductor of the band (which had drums as well), and it was clear when Ronnie's motorcade came down

This page and opposite: An unscheduled stop in Castletown, Co. Laois to be greeted by the De La Salle School brothers, pupils and tin whistle band.

the road that the best that was hoped for was maybe a slowing down of the parade and a wave of the hand from the Olympic hero. But when Ronnie took in the scene before him, he asked the driver of the Mercedes sports car in which he was riding to stop. Then he hopped out and ran toward the boys. The boys, and the Brother too, were stunned and awestricken. Then the Brother, beside himself with excitement, cried, 'Play, boys!' and, jumping up and down, he led them – solemn as little owls – in the old patriotic air, 'A Nation Once Again', which goes:

When boyhood's fire was in my blood,
I read of ancient freemen,
For Greece and Rome, who bravely stood,
Three hundred men and three men;
And then I prayed I yet might see,
Our fetters rent in twain,
And Ireland, long a province, be
A Nation once again!

As the tin whistles and drums finished, the

Brother whirled on Ronnie, now standing beside him, and, mad with excitement, implored: 'Ronnie, d'you have the gold medal!'

Ronnie dived a hand under his coat and brought out the Olympic medal, and the boys, unfreezing at last, crowded around him for a look.

'D'you see,' cried the Brother, 'd'you see the gold medal, boys! All right then, let's have a cheer: Hip, hip!'

The boys cheered lustily, and Ronnie shook hands with as many as he could and then ran back to his car, the Brother racing after him, his cassock flying, shouting with all the fervour that was left in him:

'Ah, you're very good and kind, Ronnie! You're very good and kind!'

Enthusiasm ran high all along the winding road to Dublin. Children

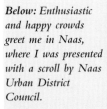

Below: Enthusiastic and happy crowds greet me in Naas, where I was presented with a scroll by Naas Urban District Council.

predominated in the crowds of the towns and villages. There were bands in some and banners in others ('Kildare Welcomes Ronnie' was one), and in between towns men ran from the fields and lorries screeched to a stop as their drivers waved and cheered. At Nenagh there was a full stop while Ronnie and his mother and father went into O'Meara's Hotel to greet the mother of Bob Tisdall, who won Ireland's last gold medal in the 1932 Olympics.

In the town of Naas there was a stop for lunch at Lawlor's Hotel. A long table had been set in the dining room for the official party, and the proprietor was wearing tails for the occasion. I was seated across from Billy Morton, and I asked him who it was who had been blowing a whistle whenever the party tarried too long on the road. In reply, Billy reached into his vest pocket and pulled out a referee's whistle which he said he carried with him at all times to deal with just such emergencies.

What, I asked Billy, had been the reaction in Dublin when the first news came of Ronnie's victory in the 1,500.

'Naturally, the city went wild,' said Billy, whose speech is reminiscent of Barry Fitzgerald, 'but to those who knew Ronnie's abilities well, it was nothing that was actually unexpected. Ronnie did a 4:05.8 mile, breaking the Irish record the first time he had ever tried it. He won it as he liked, with no trouble at all, and, mind you, it was on the grass at College Park. Now at Melbourne, Ronnie was sixteen months older and that much stronger. It stood to reason.'

Bill shoved a mouthful of potatoes and peas onto the back of his fork and went on: 'There are three things about Ronnie. One, he was born with natural ability. Two, he is able to listen and learn. Three, he has great competitive spirit. All this, plus plenty of good common sense.'

Billy chuckled.

'Get him to tell you,' he said, 'how he ran me out of the house when I first proposed that he have a go at the mile.'

As we were eating, Mr Thomas Dowling, chairman of the Naas Urban District Council, leaned over Billy Morton's shoulder and showed him a scroll he intended to present to Ronnie a little later. He said it had been composed and printed in the preceding two hours.

'Two hours!' exclaimed Billy Morton admiringly, holding the scroll up for my inspection. 'What do you say to that, Yank? Could they beat that on *Time* magazine?'

'I don't know,' said I, 'but we could beat it on *Sports Illustrated*.'

Billy realised he had identified me with the wrong magazine, but he covered his tracks quickly.

'Oh,' he said, 'I was assuming that, I was assuming that!'

Over the tea and coffee, Mr Dowling arose and presented the scroll to Ronnie, who responded briefly with just the barest hint that this was the grandest occasion of all. As final cigarettes were lighted, Captain Theo Ryan leaned over Billy Morton's shoulder and confided that, as director of the motorcade, he was planning to arrive at the

Mansion of the Lord Mayor of Dublin at 3:30.

'I think that's a mistake, Theo,' said Billy Morton. 'Four p.m. would be more like it as far as getting the crowds goes.'

'The Lord Mayor is expecting us at half three,' said Captain Ryan. 'I talked to his secretary.'

'Well, now,' said Billy Morton, who had no official status in the motorcade, 'I'm not thinking of the Lord Mayor or the Lord Mayor's secretary. My concern is for the man in the street. If I had the say, Theo, when we reach the outskirts of Dublin, I'd give the order, "Proceed at a snail's pace!"'

Captain Ryan rubbed his chin and then said, 'We'll make it half three, Billy.'

'Will you compromise, Theo,' demanded Billy desperately, 'will you compromise on quarter to four?'

Captain Ryan shook his head and moved away. Just as everyone was rising from the chairs, an elderly man wearing a moustache and an overcoat, and having no connection with the official party, arose from one of the side tables and began to speak in loud and ringing tones. Everybody sat down again.

The unscheduled speaker, it soon became plain, was not saluting Ronnie Delany, but a local hero of legend, 'the immortal Steve Conniff, who held every Irish record from one mile to 10.' As he went on and on he made it clear that, in his opinion, no man – past, present or future, and present company included – could have beaten Conniff in his prime. (I found this to be a common occurrence all during Ronnie's stay. With a little stimulation, patrons in the pubs would recall somebody out of the past who could beat Delany. With a little more stimulation, they were ready to take him on themselves, given 'a week to train and proper shoes.')

At last, with Billy Morton blowing his whistle to clear the way, the official party reached the cars, and the motorcade resumed its journey. There were no further stops scheduled until Dublin itself, but people continued to shout and wave along the roadside. Finally, Dublin's city limits were reached and cyclists by the score swung in alongside Ronnie's car and little boys and girls ran alongside and a pretty colleen climbed upon the rear bumper and rode resolutely and unsmilingly along like Joan of Arc going into battle. 'Terrific show,

Right: The motorcade slowly moves down O'Connell Street on its way to the Mansion House. Fred Moran, President of the AAUE is the front seat passenger.

Ron!' the people cried on every side, and Ronnie, when he wasn't signing autographs, waved and smiled to them. When the car pulled up in front of the Lord Mayor's Mansion the crowd swept over the lawn, and the police, in the good-humoured way of Dublin Guards, cleared a path for Ronnie, who raced up the steps to shake the outstretched hand of the Lord Mayor of Dublin, Robert Briscoe.

'It is my great privilege,' said the Lord Mayor when the crowd had quieted down, 'to be in office when a Dublin citizen has brought so much credit not only to Dublin but to Ireland by his wonderful accomplishment. It gives me the greatest of pleasure, Ronnie Delany, to extend to you the warmest congratulations of all our citizens.'

He stepped away from the microphone, and Ronnie took it over.

'My Lord Mayor,' he said easily, as though he were accustomed to speaking from the steps of the Lord Mayor's Mansion every day of the week, 'ladies and gentlemen, young boys and young girls. Thank you for this wonderful reception. I thought I might have created a bit of a stir, but I never expected anything like this. I sincerely hope that in the future I will be able to bring further

Above: Cyclists swing in beside the motorcade as it passes through the streets of Dublin.

Bottom: The maestro himself – my friend Billy Morton of Clonliffe Harriers.

honours to Dublin and to Ireland.'

THE GRAND RECEPTION

Then everyone went into the Lord Mayor's Mansion for a reception. It was a grand affair, with drinks for everyone's taste. Ronnie's father, Patrick A. Delany, who is a customs official, stood chatting with the Lord Mayor and other notables, and Ronnie himself sat on a sofa talking to Eamon Kinsella, the hurdler of the Irish Olympic team.

A little later when Ronnie was talking to another group, a Dublin pressman came up and asked him who the man (Kinsella) on the sofa was. Ronnie looked at him

Above:
The Right
Honourable Lord
Mayor of Dublin,
Robert Briscoe,
presents me with a
beautiful Waterford
Glass vase at the
Mansion House.

incredulously. 'Well,' he said, the colour going out of his face as it does when he is annoyed, 'if you, as a Dublin pressman don't know who he is, then I'm certainly not going to tell you.' And he turned away.

But, altogether, it was a day that no small irritation could spoil. The next morning, refreshed by ten hours sleep, Ronnie drove in his hired car from his home, a brick house in a row of identical houses on St. John's Road in Sandymount, a suburb of Dublin, to the General Post Office on O'Connell Street. There, in the studios of Radio Éireann, he sat down with Philip Green, the sports broadcaster, and told the story of his victory in the 1,500 metres at Melbourne as it had never been told all the long way home.

That afternoon I visited Ronnie at home, and his mother served tea and biscuits and buttered bread in the parlour with its fireplace and piano and comfortable furniture and Ronnie's trophies everywhere. Ronnie's father brought out some of the letters he had received after Ronnie's victory, and among the letters was one from Eamon De Valera, the former head of the Irish government, who lives not far

Left: With Eamon Kinsella at the Lord Mayor's reception in the Mansion House.

away from the Delanys. In his letter Mr De Valera compared Ronnie's great victory to the exploits of Matt Donovan, the legendary Irish ploughman celebrated for his ability to plough a furrow straighter than a straight line. Like Matt, said Mr De Valera, Ronnie had won 'for the credit of the little village.'

I remembered to ask Ronnie if he had, indeed, ordered Billy Morton from the house when he first suggested the running of the mile in a Dublin meet.

'Ah, yes,' laughed Ronnie, 'I remember, I told him I didn't want to hear any such nonsense, and I sent him out of the house. Well, Billy went over in a flash to see Daddy and when Daddy came home he asked me to run it and I refused again. He insisted and I said, "That's all very well for you to say, Da, but I've got to do the running." Well, Da kept at me and finally I decided to run the thing.

'But the funny thing was that Elisabeth and I had been dancing

every night for a week when the day of the race came and I was pretty tired. But didn't it lash rain and the race have to be postponed for two days? By that time I was well rested and ran the 4:05.8 for a new Irish record. And I felt very good doing it, too.'

Ronnie's brother Joe came in with his pretty, rosy-cheeked girlfriend Markie O'Callaghan, and they presented Ronnie with a big leather-bound scrapbook stamped in gold letters: 'Ronnie's Great Day'. Furthermore, knowing how busy Ronnie would be with his studies and his running, they volunteered to keep it up for him. Ronnie thanked them profusely and then remembered he had something himself to show them all. He went and got it, and what was it but a black tie embroidered with a golden wreath, in the

centre of which appeared the legend '4 M.M.' Ronnie said Roger Bannister had sent it, and others like it to the eight other four-minute milers.

Then it was time for Ronnie to go, for he had a date with Elisabeth, of course, and at the door he waved and said, 'God bless.'

Ronnie and Elisabeth were on the go all the time. One night they went to see Bing Crosby and Frank Sinatra in *High Society* and another night to *Oklahoma!* At the latter, Ronnie was recognised as he came in, and the whole audience started cheering, and nothing would do but for him to go up on the stage and say a few words. Afterward, the manager came to his seat and whispered that he had better leave a few minutes early to avoid a mob scene. Another evening Ronnie took Elisabeth to see the variety bill at the Gaiety and he said 'it gave me a queer feeling' when, in one of the skits, the comedian kept telling his wife to run and get this and that until she finally exclaimed: 'It's always run here and run there. Who do you think I am — Ronnie Delany?'

One night I invited Ronnie and Elisabeth to dinner and the theatre, and they selected the Russell Hotel for dinner and the Gate Theatre, where *The Importance of Being Earnest*, by another famous Dubliner, was playing. At the Russell the menu was in French, of all things, and Ronnie solved that by ordering 'thick soup, steak and trifle for dessert.' At the Gate, Lord Longford himself, the producer, came up and congratulated Ronnie and bowed low to Elisabeth.

Afterward, Ronnie proposed a sightseeing tour of Dublin in the rain, and as we drove along, Elisabeth spoke of her art studies and made deprecating mention of the amateur theatrical company she played in.

'Ah,' said Ronnie, 'you're too modest altogether. Didn't the critic who saw you in *Arms and the Man* say you were another Siobhán McKenna?'

We passed by the shops of Grafton Street and then, a little later, the old section of Dublin known as 'The Coombe'. As Ronnie pointed it out, Elisabeth sang the Dublin classic:

I'm a fine buxom widow,
I live in a spot,
In Dublin they call it the Coombe;

My shops and my stalls are laid out on the street,
And my palace consists of one room.

Ronnie joined in the chorus:

You may travel from Clare,
To the County Kildare,
From Francis Street on to Macroom,
But where would you see,
A fine widow like me?
Biddy Mulligan, the pride of the Coombe.

They have the Irish gift of laughter. When Ronnie won at Melbourne, Elisabeth wrote him an airmail letter in which she said (among other things): 'Not bad for a grade B 100-yarder' – which was Ronnie's first rating as a schoolboy runner.

Sometimes Elisabeth would tell of places she had gone and dances she had been to while Ronnie was at school. At such times they have a little game they play. At the end of her story, Elisabeth says, 'And then this question followed.' And Ronnie always takes the cue and asks, 'Who took you?'

Their understanding is no secret in Dublin. Ronnie received a Christmas card from a girl in America, and a Dublin college student, working extra in the post office for the holidays, scrawled over the girl's home address on the back of the envelope, 'And what will Liz MacArthur say to this?'

RONNIE ON RUNNING

Ronnie visited two hospitals during his stay at home. One was St Mary's for crippled children at Cappagh, and the other was St Augustine's for retarded children at Blackrock.

In the car, driving out, the subject turned (as it did invariably elsewhere) to the subject of running, and I asked Ronnie to repeat some of the things he had touched on during the flight from New York.

I recalled that he was booed in Madison Square Garden last winter for running only as fast as he needed to and on competing against the clock, Ronnie said:

'I think the sport of running is in the competition. And the competition is not against the clock, but against another human being like yourself.

'Now when I run against a man I enjoy it. But if I were to set up a timepiece there and try to beat it, I wouldn't get enjoyment out of it at all. The thrill of running, the pleasure of running to me is not in making records and getting your name flashed around the papers, but winning races and winning them by beating another man in a fair run.

'Like if I run a four-minute mile and I'm running against fellows who can only run 4:12, the spectacle isn't there, the thrill isn't there. You look at a man, you can't tell what time he's running. It's only afterwards you get the pleasure from the time. I remember the moderator of athletics at Catholic University School in Dublin, Father Lonergan. When I was eighteen, I asked him before one race, "Father, will I have a go at the record?" He said, "Ronnie, don't do anything of the sort. Run to win your race." I never forgot that advice and I've been following it ever since.'

Of the tension he feels before a race, Ronnie said:

'Before every meeting, no matter how small or how big it is, I get this terrible sensation in my stomach, that terrible nervous feeling. Sometimes it's worse than others. In the Olympics, I found I was controlling it very well. I felt that my mind was in command of my body at Melbourne. But usually the feeling is that you can't run an inch and the last thing you want to do is run. Except for the Olympics, I've never been able to acquire any great confidence in my running just before a race.'

I reminded Ronnie that John Landy said that if anybody ever ran a 3:55 mile, he – Ronnie – would probably be the one to do it.

'It's all a matter of mind over body,' said Ronnie. 'A few years ago, no one could run a four-minute mile. Now ten men have done it. A couple of us are very young. I'm the youngest, twenty-one, and Brian Hewson's only twenty-three. None of us has reached his peak, the peak supposedly coming around age twenty-five. Definitely we're going to improve in the next few years, everything being in order and

God willing. We're all going to improve, and the only way we can improve is not in style but in going down, going a little faster. Well, if we're running 3:59 now, we can run 3:58 next year maybe and 3:57 the year after and then who knows where we will stop.'

At St Mary's hospital, Ronnie went from bed to bed, making sure that he missed no one. Some of the children wore little paper hats that the Sisters had made for them. One had printed on it: 'Welcome, Ronnie. It was kind of you to come and visit us.' A little boy on crutches wore a hat that read: 'I'll run you, Ronnie.'

At St Augustine's, in the home for retarded children, Ronnie appeared with Santa Claus and made a little speech and then got down on the floor and showed the boys how to work their toys, as a band from the village played Christmas carols. At the end of the visit one of the Brothers called for a cheer, and then everyone stood at attention for the Irish national anthem.

'I'll Run You Ronnie',
says the hat of the
courageous little patient
when I visited St
Mary's Hospital,
Cappagh.

One afternoon Billy Morton invited the leading citizens of Dublin, including the Lord Mayor himself, to a special meeting in Room 318 of the Gresham Hotel. Billy had a buffet laid on, and plenty of good drinks, and came right to the heart of the matter, which was that he had purchased a wonderful tract of land at Santry on the road to the Dublin airport and wanted the distinguished gentlemen present to help him raise the money to build the first cinder running track in all Ireland. Then he called upon Ronnie to say a few words. Ronnie got up and said:

'My Lord Mayor and gentlemen. Naturally, I am very pleased at the interest my victory in the Olympics has aroused here at home. But, gentlemen, while it's all very well for people to be interested and be clapping me on the back and shaking my hand, what I would really like them to do to show their appreciation for my little prize at Melbourne is something constructive, and the constructive thing I want to see is the building of a cinder track.

'In my own belief, gentlemen, there are ten or twelve other O'Reillys and Kinsellas and Delanys around the country, perhaps even walking the streets of Dublin at this moment. These young people would run if they had the facilities to run. Now we, as athletes, can buy our shoes, we can learn from fine coaches like Jack Sweeney, Louis Vandendries and Captain Theo Ryan. But we can't build a cinder track ourselves. That's up to men like you. Billy Morton has taken a wonderful step in acquiring a site that I believe to be the finest in the world.

'Gentlemen, I have found to my own detriment that I can't train on grass alone. When you get into big-time athletics, you've got to have big-time facilities to work with. Our boys can't be expected to compete against the other athletes of the world under the present unfavourable conditions.'

Ronnie looked around at the distinguished citizens present, their mouths open at the poise and assurance of this twenty-one-year-old. Then Ronnie closed off his speech by stating emphatically:

'This cinder track is not something for me personally, it isn't for Billy Morton personally. This is something for all Ireland, something for our capital city of Dublin to be proud of – our own cinder track. Thank you, gentlemen.' As Ronnie sat down, the Lord Mayor got up and announced that he was not a rich man. But, he said, he would like to start the ball rolling with a personal contribution of £25. The upshot was that a total of £51 was pledged then and there and promises made of full support for Billy's cinder-track scheme 'The amount collected,' said Billy Morton afterward, 'represents a profit of 100% for the occasion. Which isn't bad at this stage of the game.'

MR COSTELLO LAUGHS

Another afternoon Ronnie and the entire Olympic team were escorted by Lord Killanin and the other officials to Government Buildings to meet the Irish Prime Minister, John A. Costello, TD.

Now, it must be borne in mind (as Ronnie himself explained to me) that Mr Costello is a man with great problems on his mind, economic and political. Perhaps (said Ronnie) this explains why he is renowned in Ireland for never smiling.

Mr Costello greeted the athletes in a friendly way, but he maintained his dour expression. One of the photographers was bold enough to call out, 'Oh, come now, sir, let's have a smile.'

Mr Costello tried, but he couldn't manage it. Then Ronnie leaned over to him and (thinking of the prime minister's great burdens) said:

'Sure, what have you got to smile about, Mr Costello?'

Ronnie (he said later) recoiled in horror at the presumption 'of an upstart like me' in speaking so.

But what did Mr Costello do but throw back his head and laugh heartily and say, 'How right you are, Delany!'

Dubliners cultivate the art of public speaking (although most of them, like Ronnie Delany, seem to be born with it), and the dinners given for the Olympic heroes provided rare opportunities for oratorical flourishes.

Lord Killanin, as president, presided over the dinner given by the Olympic Council of Ireland at the Dolphin Hotel, and opened the affair with a toast to the President of Ireland. The room was cold and draughty at first, but soon it was warm with the cordiality of the speakers. Every speech had wit and eloquence, and Chief Superintendent (of the police) Patrick Carroll even succeeded in making a roll call of distinguished guests sound like an epic poem. He included in his tributes one to Billy Morton, 'whose enthusiasm comes in bucketsful,' and I sat up at this, for a Dublin man had confided to me that on certain athletic questions Mr Carroll and Mr Morton were 'at daggers drawn'.

Right: Dad, Mum and Joe look at a wired photo from Melbourne of the 1,500m finish on the morning of 1 December 1956.

But it was Colonel F. A. Ahern, who has brought many an Irish jumping team to the National Horse Show in New York's Madison Square Garden, who reached the pinnacle of eloquence for the evening. A handsome ramrod of a man, wearing his army uniform, Colonel Ahern paid tribute to the gallant horses and the gallant men who had represented Ireland in the equestrian events of the Olympics at Stockholm. Then, his rich and vibrant voice quivering with emotion, he turned to Ireland's greatest hero of the day and said:

'Ronnie Delany, you have raised the heart of every Irishman at home and abroad.'

Looking out over the guests again, he went on:

'The question is asked: who is responsible for this fine boy's success? Who is to be credited with his training?'

He paused and dropped his voice to a whisper.

'I think I know.' He raised his soldierly arm slowly and pointed.

'There sits his mother. There sits his father.'

He waited, then turned back to Ronnie.

'Oh, Ronnie,' he said, 'hold fast to the ideals learned at that dear mother's knee. Remain steadfast in the principles instilled in you by your devoted father. Keep that excellent modesty that has been such a credit to Ireland. Do these things and I promise you, Ronnie, that the long and glorious path ahead shall be strewn with golden laurels.'

The hit of the evening at the AAU dinner, presided over by President Fred Moran at the Shelbourne Hotel a few nights later, was Ronnie's father, Patrick A. Delany, looking as distinguished with his silver-grey hair and athletic physique as Colonel Ahern himself.

'This,' said Mr Delany, 'is my day, this is my hour of glory. I am not known for anything I have done myself, I am merely known as the father of Ronnie Delany.'

He spoke of the great Irish patriots, Parnell and Emmet and O'Connell, and the words by which they are best remembered. He said that perhaps Winston Churchill would be remembered best for his tribute to the RAF in the Battle of Britain: 'Never was so much owed by so many to so few.' Mr Delany paused, and the room was breathless.

'And now,' he went on, 'since this is my hour, I should like to say the words for which I hope I will be remembered.'

'Never,' he said, holding his head high, 'never were so many made so proud and so happy ... by one!'

There was a standing ovation.

Irish banquets never fail to provide a neat balance between sentiment and hilarity, and a little later all the guests (about one hundred) were joining in singing the great sporting song, 'Bould Thady Quill', the chorus of which goes:

For gambling and bowling, for football and courting,
Or draining a jorum as fast as you'd fill,
In all your days roving, you'd find none so jovial
As our Muskerry sportsman, that's Bould Thady Quill.

After that, Ronnie himself was persuaded to go to the piano and play the only song he knows by heart, 'I'll Be Loving You Eternally'. When he had finished, the Lord Mayor (the Lord Mayor was everywhere, it seemed) came up to Ronnie and said that the song was his favourite as well. He also confided that if ever Ronnie wanted to stand for public office to let him know.

Could anything, in the way of entertainment, have topped all that? Ah, yes, indeed. Billy Morton, the man who first proposed that Ronnie Delany try running the mile, got up and sang 'Mother Machree' with power and authority and followed that by dancing the grandest buck-

and-wing that Dublin had seen in many a day.

LUCK OF THE IRISH

Fate had one more favour waiting for Ronnie Delany. Just as he was saying his last goodbye to Elisabeth MacArthur and the both of them wishing for just a few more minutes, Liam Boyd, the TWA man in Dublin, called on the telephone and said the weather had held up Ronnie's flight and he would have to spend another twenty-four hours at home.

Last week, Ronnie Delany, the Dublin boy, was back at Villanova, studying, training and directing traffic at the Sunday Masses at St Thomas' Church to earn his $5 weekly spending money. And the County Clare man (who had found his first cousins and stood in the room where his father was born) was back at his desk at *Sports Illustrated*. Before parting in New York, the Dublin boy had said, 'Was it not the grandest trip you ever had?' And the Clare man had replied, 'Ah, it was, it was.'

My dad with the debonair and likeable Gerald Holland of Sports Illustrated.

THE MAGIC SHOVEL

When Gerald Holland wrote the story of my homecoming for *Sports Illustrated*, he never expected to be back in Ireland for a second time in less than six months. How this came about is an extraordinary story of Ireland at that time.

Gerald Holland had a curious phone call from a reader of the magazine shortly after my homecoming story appeared. This turned out to be no ordinary reader, but one Bernard Patrick McDonough, a wealthy West Virginia businessman, whose interests included the largest shovel making factory in the world. Mr McDonough told Gerald that he wanted to find out at first hand what he could do by way of investment to improve the economic prosperity in Ireland. They discovered after a few meetings that they shared a mutual interest in Ireland. Their acquaintance developed to the point where Gerald came to Ireland with McDonough on a reconnaissance trip.

I am not going to tell the story of what happened next. I leave that to Gerald for he wrote a fascinating story on the immediate outcome, which *Sports Illustrated* published in two successive issues of the magazine in July 1957.

It is remarkable that my Olympic achievement was generating so much interest in Ireland. And it was timely too for the fledgling Irish Industrial Authority (IDA) was actively seeking investment in Ireland. No one would ever have thought that my golden run would trigger the development of Co. Clare's tourism industry.

It was six more years before Bernard McDonough the self-made millionaire met Brendan O'Regan the dynamic CEO of Shannon in mid-1962. O'Regan was a remarkable man whose remit at the time extended to aviation, tourism, industrial promotion, regional development, or in simple language, selling the midwest.

At that time McDonough and his companies were reportedly thinking of setting up shovel, ball bearing and furniture manufacturing plants in Ireland with investments running into millions of dollars. But the eccentric McDonough was turned off time after time by what he perceived as rip-off prices and so forth.

It took the creative genius of Brendan O'Regan to suggest an entirely opposite area for investment – the emerging tourism sector. What followed is history, but worth repeating.

Initially McDonough bought Dromoland Castle from Sir Donough O'Brien, the sixteenth Lord Inchquin. Dromoland was fit for a king. It brought new life to the Shannon region, providing employment while attracting a new elite tourist to the area. The Dromoland venture was followed subsequently by the outstanding Clare Inn Hotel nearby.

Two great entrepreneurs had formed a business relationship based on trust. When Brendan O'Regan wanted a hotel at Shannon Airport a deal was struck with B. P. McDonough. He built the International Hotel while O'Regan provided the managers and staff and established a permanent home for the Shannon College of Hotel Management. McDonough would then go on to build the Limerick Inn and was often in the headlines because of a long-running dispute with Clare County Council planning officials.

It was not until after the death of Bernard McDonough that Dromoland Castle and the Clare Inn were sold in 1987. Previously he had sold the International Hotel at Shannon to Aer Rianta. This became the starting point for the Great Southern Hotel Group.

My meetings with Mr McDonough were infrequent. In the early summer of 1958, the year I would graduate from Villanova, he flew me down to Parkersburg, West Virginia in his private Cessna. I had dinner with his friends and family that evening in the Country Club. Next day I visited the shovel factory, furniture plant and some other of his enterprises in the area.

Somewhere along the line I was 'interviewed' in his own whimsical way 'as to my interest in working for one of his enterprises'. Mr McDonough came straight to the point when he asked me how important running was in my life and how much time did training and racing take up. I could already see that I was dealing with a single-minded and tough taskmaster. I was twenty-three years old and I decided I had better explain that I planned to continue my running career into the future and that it did take up a lot of time. Time for training, travel and competitions.

We were alike in one way. We both relied on instinct and I was clearly not right for the job he had in mind. It was one of those 'either or' situations again. I would have had to make the same commitment to working for him as I had to my running career. But my enduring memory of Bernard P. McDonough is of the grandson of a Galway man who began the trend of Irish American investment in Ireland. This is his proud legacy today. I am so pleased to be part of his story and to have been instrumental in awakening his interest in Ireland.

Gerald's journalistic style is pure 1950's reportage. It gives today's readers a fascinating insight into the perceptions Americans then had of Ireland. (Some might say things have not changed that much, particularly around 17 March each year.)

...But Not for 'Distance' Ron Delany Talks Like He Runs

By EARL EBY

THERE ARE few athletes throughout the world who are as versatile as miler Ron Delaney.

In addition to his running career in which he set a new Olympic record in the 1,500 meters, ran the mile under four minutes three times ad holds the indoor world record for the distance of 4:02.5, the Irishman is somewhat of a champ in other fields.

For instance, he is one of the most glib extemporaneous after dinner speakers in the athletic world. He can be so incisive in rejoinder that one wonders why he didn't continue in law at Villanova instead of in dramatics.

When Ron was in the vicinity of San Francisco three years ago to compete in a special mile race, he became somewhat annoyed at the boasting of his California host.

"We grow the biggest thi[ngs] and that. We have the best this[...] Where can this climate be mat[...] ed?'" the Californian pounded [...] Delany's ear.

He's a Good Thinker

AT A DINNER follow[...] race which Delany won in sub-four-minute time, called upon to speak. "I was informed [...] "I've been hearing much about this state[...] the Irishman began. "But there is one thin[...] everything. But [...] [...]cked up two sm[...]

Ron Delany
Irish Wit

MR McDONOUGH'S
MAGIC SHOVEL

How Sports Illustrated*'s description of miler Ronnie Delany's welcome home to Ireland inspired a certain telephone call and set off a whole series of adventures involving people, shovels, aircraft and the fate of old Erin*

by GERALD HOLLAND

For the second time in six months, thanks to the great Irish miler, Ronnie Delany, I found myself high over the Atlantic, staring out the plane window, looking down on the clouds that hid the sea below. I had tried to sleep in a berth forward, but I couldn't. There was too much to think about; large, wonderful thoughts that grew in the mystical beauty of the night. Suspended in space and time, I gave myself freely to a dream. The son of a County Clare man, I felt that I was returning to the Old Country in the vanguard of a crusade to rescue modern Ireland from the troubles that sorely beset her. Savouring the fancy, I thought back over the way in which it had all come about.

One day I received a telephone call from a man who introduced himself as Bernard P. McDonough of Parkersburg, West Virginia. He said he had read *Sports Illustrated*'s account of Ronnie Delany's welcome home to Ireland last December. He was calling me, he went on, as one who had recently visited over there and, presumably, had more up-to-date impressions of the country than his own.

Mr McDonough said that, as the grandson of a County Galway man, he was distressed by reports that he read about Ireland's economic plight. He understood that young people were leaving the country in great numbers because of lack of employment opportunities. He had thought about the problem so much, Mr McDonough said, that now he was seriously considering starting some kind of business in Ireland in order to give jobs and perhaps set an example that other American businessmen might follow.

I asked Mr McDonough what his business interests were.

He said he had a number of interests, including the largest shovel factory in the world.

I asked him to repeat that,

Mr McDonough did and explained that the largest shovel factory in the world was the O. Ames Company of Parkersburg, founded in 1774, presently turning out 10,000 shovels (1,800 varieties) every day.

Did that mean, I asked, that he proposed to start a shovel factory in Ireland?

Possibly so, he said,

We chatted on and discovered we had a lot in common. My mother, Margaret O'Connor, was born in West Virginia, not 60 miles from where Mr McDonough was now speaking. Moreover, it developed, both Mr McDonough's grandfather and mine had helped to build the Baltimore and Ohio Railroad through West Virginia, and, we agreed, had almost certainly done so with Ames shovels.

Abruptly, Mr McDonough asked me the question that was the real reason for his call.

'Tell me frankly out of what you have observed,' he said. 'Will the Irish in Ireland work?'

I asked him to hold the phone. I got up and closed the office door. Returning to my desk, I picked up the phone and said:

'Mr McDonough, that is a question I would not care to discuss over the long distance wire. It is a very delicate question. Let me say simply that there is a lot of Guinness Stout brewed in Ireland, for one thing, and somebody must have to work to brew it.'

Mr McDonough agreed that the question could not be answered offhand. We came to a decision: on Mr McDonough's next visit to New York, we would have lunch and confer further. Or if, by chance, I was ever in the vicinity of Parkersburg, I would call him.

Events moved swiftly. Not long after my first talk with Mr McDonough, a fortuitous circumstance sent me to West Virginia, and I found myself being ushered into McDonough's office. As I entered, he was talking into a box on his desk to a ship's captain who was in the Gulf of Mexico bound for Venezuela, where Mr McDonough has a marine business. As I waited for the conversation to be concluded, I observed Mr McDonough out of the corner of my eye and judged him (correctly) to be in his early

60s, a man of average height, with thinning, but still brown hair, the suspicion of an Irish twinkle in his eyes, a habit of raising his eyebrows and tightening his lips when he was listening and half smiling when he was speaking. When the ship-to-shore talk ended, Mr McDonough jumped up, shook hands and announced that he was taking the rest of the day off to show me around.

WHERE SHOVELS RULE

It was a great day. We toured a number of plants, but the most astonishing was the O. Ames Company, the shovel factory. In my city man's ignorance, I had believed the shovel to be obsolete. Now, standing on the floor of the Ames main plant, I had the feeling that shovels rule the world. There were shovels everywhere amid the din and clatter of the machinery; there was every kind of shovel imaginable: shovels to dig holes for telephone poles; wide shovels, narrow shovels, long-handled and short-handled shovels, even a shovel to shovel fish. Shovels were being moulded, hammered, pounded, stamped, shined; everything that can be done to a shovel was being done.

I stopped at one assembly line to watch a man whose job it was to stand before a parade of shovels, and as each one reached him to take a nail in his left hand and hit it a single blow with the hammer he held in his right. He had one chance and one blow before the shovel moved on. If he missed, the whole operation would be thrown off. In secret dismay, I thought of a cousin of mine over in Ireland and how he might, given just such a job, exclaim at precisely the wrong instant: 'Now wait till I spit on me hands!' Chaos would surely result.

I moved along and watched another man. He faced a battery of machines arranged in a semicircle. One machine delivered a molten shovel which the man took and, whirling and posturing like José Greco, the Spanish dancer, he thrust it in the other machines, one after the other, to stamp and shape it. His final act was to fling the shovel from him in a gesture as graceful as a ballet figure; then, without pause, he started all over again. I could hear my Irish cousin as he went through this procedure just once; 'Ah life's too short! T'hell with it!'

As we started for the executive dining room, Mr McDonough pointed to a spot on the factory floor where he had worked as a boy for 15 cent an hour.

At lunch with the production men and some of the sales people, Mr McDonough raised the question of manufacturing shovels in Ireland. He mentioned that he knew of a factory in Galway that might be acquired and modernised. The production men said it was possible to manufacture shovels in Ireland, all right, but pointed out that both wood and metal would have to be imported and the finished product would have to be exported, the Irish domestic market being inadequate for a profitable operation. The place to build a shovel factory outside the United States, said one production man, was Puerto Rico. Mr McDonough nodded and the subject was dropped.

A great depression came over me at the mention of Puerto Rico, and I could not shake it even after we drove out to the Ohio River and went for a cruise on one of the tugboats operated by a sand and gravel company Mr McDonough owns. As I stood at the rail of the tug, looking at the green banks of the historic Ohio of Lincoln and Boone, I was reminded suddenly of the River Shannon. I turned to my host:

'Mr McDonough,' I said, 'coming to Parkersburg has been a most rewarding experience, I have been fascinated by the shovel manufacturing process, and I have always wanted to ride on a tugboat. This is one of the great days of my life.'

Mr McDonough appeared to be mildly embarrassed by the intensity of my gratitude.

'And to whom do I owe thanks for this delightful adventure? To you, of course, but other than you, to whom? To some Puerto Rican sprinter? To some Puerto Rican putter of the shot, some pole vaulter, hurdler, jumper?'

Mr McDonough took off his hat and waved it to the captain at the wheel, signalling a return to the sand and gravel company dock.

'We are here together at the rail of this tugboat,' I said firmly, 'thanks to no Puerto Rican, but thanks to the greatest runner of the mile in all Ireland's history, Ronald Michael Delany. Had he not won in the Olympics, I would not have written the story about him and had I not written the story about him you would not have called me in the first place.'

'What are you driving at?' asked Mr McDonough.

'The talk at lunch about starting a factory in Puerto Rico,' I said. 'I hope it will not divert you from your plan to help Ireland.'

Mr McDonough raised a hand to shield his eyes as the tugboat turned into the sun. 'We'll see,' he said 'We'll see.'

Back at the dock we got into Mr McDonough's car and drove to a sandlot where his son, Bernard Jr., 16, was pitching in a pickup game. We watched for a while, then drove to Mr McDonough's home and met his daughter, Mary, who is 14. As we sat on a side porch with some refreshments, Mrs McDonough, blonde and slender, a former schoolteacher in Parkersburg, drove up and joined us. She had been out at the country club practising the Ben Hogan golf lessons. Mr McDonough proposed that the three of us go back to the club for dinner.

THE PROPER THING TO DO

After dinner we sat for a long time discussing Ireland. Mr McDonough said that, seriously speaking, the proper way to go about starting an enterprise in Ireland was to send a team of experts in to survey the manufacturing possibilities and then to study their recommendations. 'However,' said Mr McDonough as we parted at the end of the evening, 'it might be useful to fly over there some weekend and talk to a few people and get the feel of the place again. I'll give you a call one of these days, and we'll run over for two or three days.'

Back in New York, heartland of doubletalk, where 'Let's lunch one day' may well mean 'I hope I never see your face again,' I decided to close the book on a pleasant adventure. I reported to my superior for assignment and was promptly sent to New Jersey to cover a luncheon at which the guest of honour was a dog, an English setter named Rock Falls Colonel.

Two days later I received an airmail special delivery from Mr McDonough in which he said that he found himself free for the coming weekend and had taken the liberty of making two reservations for Ireland on TWA Flight No. 862 leaving Idlewild Airport in New York at 2:30 p.m. on Thursday. He said he would fly to New York in his own plane, a twin-engine Cessna. 'If convenient,' wrote Mr McDonough, 'meet me at the TWA check-in counter one hour before departure time.'

Right: At Santry Stadium with my lifelong friends from sport after the 'Miracle Mile' in August 1958: Merv Lincoln (front), Albie Thomas, Herb Elliott and Murray Halberg.

I picked up the telephone and called the New York law firm of Satterlee, Warfield & Stephens and asked to speak to one of the partners, Mr Francis W. H. Adams. I was calling Mr Adams for two reasons: 1) he is a member of the board of directors of the American Irish Historical Society and so has certain contacts with the Old Country; and two he is a hard man to startle.

Happily, Mr Adams was free for lunch. I waited until we had finished our fricassee of chicken to bring him up date on what had been happening. I showed him Mr McDonough's letter. Mr Adams blanched, but the colour returned to his face almost immediately. He cleared his throat.

'This project,' he said, 'strikes me as being eminently sensible. I will confess that, at first impact, the teaming of an American industrialist and a sportswriter for the purpose you describe does seem a trifle irregular. However upon reflection, I can see that your recent trip to Ireland with Ronnie Delany may have equipped you with certain information and contacts that will assist Mr McDonough in his larger plan. Suffice it to say, I shall be happy to support the enterprise in any way I can. I think, first of all the Irish Government should be alerted. I'll get off an airmail letter this afternoon and send you a copy.'

Mr Adams was as good as his word. At 4:10 p.m. a Verifax copy of his letter was laid on my desk. It was addressed to the Irish Industrial Authority, a Government agency in Dublin. It described the purpose of our visit and identified Mr McDonough as 'an important American industrialist and a man of substance,' and mentioned that I was a sportswriter. Mr Adams concluded his letter saying that we would be available at the Gresham Hotel in Dublin on the following Saturday.

On Thursday, the day of our scheduled take-off for Ireland, I was up at 6 a.m. although the plane did not leave until 2:30 in the afternoon. I was thinking hard. Being realistic about it, I had to admit that the weekend in Ireland, by itself, could have no lasting benefits to the Irish economy. But I felt that even a weekend could be turned to Ireland's advantage if somehow it could be made symbolic of greater things to come. I chewed the word symbolic and reduced it to symbol. If a symbol could be found.

Suddenly struck, I hurried to my file of *Sports Illustrated* and turned to the January 21 issue with the story of Ronnie Delany's homecoming after his Olympic victory. Feverishly I searched for the paragraph I only half remembered. And there it was: Ronnie himself addressed a meeting of Dublin's leading citizens, a meeting that had been called by Ireland's foremost promoter of amateur athletics, Billy Morton.

'My Lord Mayor and gentlemen' [said Ronnie], 'Naturally, I am very pleased at the interest my victory in the Olympics has aroused here at home. But, gentlemen, while it's all very well for people to be interested and be clapping me on the back and shaking my hand, what I would really like them to do to show their appreciation for my little prize at Melbourne is something constructive, and the constructive thing I want to see is the building of a cinder track. Billy Morton has taken a wonderful step in acquiring a site that I believe to be the finest in the world. Gentlemen, I have found to my own detriment that I cannot train on grass alone. ... This cinder track is not something for me personally, it isn't for Billy Morton personally. This is something for all Ireland, something for our capital city, Dublin, to be proud of – our own cinder track.'

I had my idea. I hurried to the telephone (it was round 9:30 a.m.) and called TWA headquarters at Idlewild; asked for Mr James Cahill, a young man whose forebears came from County Clare. He was free for lunch.

In the Brass Rail restaurant at the airport, I waited until we had finished our pastrami sandwiches before saying to Mr Cahill: 'Jim, I wonder if you would be good enough to consult with your people and sound them out on their willingness to cooperate in a project aimed at promoting understanding and friendship between two nations.' Mr Cahill took a sip of coffee.

'What two nations?' he said. 'The US,' I said, 'and Free Ireland.' Mr Cahill fumbled for a cigarette. I held out a match for him. He took a deep drag and blew the smoke at the ceiling. 'I don't have to consult with my people,' he said, 'to answer your question in general terms. Of course my company is always ready and eager to promote friendship and understanding between the two countries you have named. What, specifically, would you ask us to do?'

I waited until the waitress had taken our plates away. Then I leaned forward.

'Jim,' I said lowering my voice, 'the details of this matter have not been settled as yet. But what I might ask you to do is fly a shovel to Ireland.'

Some smoke from Mr Cahill's cigarette caught in his throat at that moment, and he took a fit of coughing. I raised up in my chair and signalled the waitress for a refill of the water glasses. The waitress hurried over with a pitcher and, after taking a sip, Mr Cahill recovered his composure. 'Excuse me,' he said.

'As I was saying, Jim,' I went on. 'This matter would involve flying a shovel to Ireland. I don't mean air express or anything like that. I mean that the shovel would have to be handed ever to the steward or purser of the plane and handled by him personally. Then, at Shannon Airport, there would have to be somebody waiting with a fast motor-car to take the shovel to Dublin, where your man there would take it and deliver it to Mr Billy Morton at No. 10 Berkeley Street. Or maybe it should be delivered to the Lord Mayor's Mansion. I'll let you know.'

I leaned back in my chair.

'Am I making sense, James?' I asked.

Mr Cahill nodded, staring at his hands. Then he looked up and said:

'Would it be out of order for me to ask what flying a shovel to Ireland has to do with promoting understanding and friendship between the two nations?'

I shook my head.

'I cannot tell you any more at this present time, Jim,' I said. 'What it boils down to is this: if a shovel is delivered to you here at Idlewild in the next few days, you just hold on to it until you hear from me. Clear?'

'Well,' said Mr Cahill, 'No. But I'll go along with this thing in the hope that it will become clear later on.'

'Believe me, it will, James,' I said.

I called for the check and we walked out of the Brass Rail and over to the TWA check-in counter. Mr McDonough was there waiting. In a little while our flight was announced and we went aboard the plane and soon were out over the sea, flying nonstop to Ireland.

Thinking back over all this on the plane, I had fallen asleep in my seat. Now I felt myself being shaken. I opened my eyes and there was Mr McDonough, dressed and shaved.

Left: Dublin's Lord Mayor, Robert Briscoe, visits Villanova University and presents me with the magnificent 'Flame of Faith' trophy from the Waterford Glass workers, 24 April 1957.

'We're landing at Shannon,' he said.

I looked out the window and there it was rushing up at me: the wonderful green of the old Country. The Irish Adventure was beginning.

THE MAGIC BEGINS TO WORK

A whirlwind tour of Ireland completes the spadework of weekend economic survey and makes secure forever the place of the shovel in the history of Irish athletics.

by GERALD HOLLAND

At Shannon Airport where a driver was waiting with a Vauxhall sedan to drive us wherever we wanted to go, I decided to tell Mr McDonough something I had been thinking about on the plane, 'Mr McDonough,' I said, 'now that we are on Irish soil, I wonder if I might presume to think of myself not only as an American sportswriter, but as a consultant on Irish affairs and, if you will, a sort of public-relations counsellor. Have you any objections?'

Mr McDonough held up a hand.

'Please,' he said, 'think of yourself in any way that gives you pleasure.'

'Thank you,' I said. 'Now I feel free to bring up a public relations thing. Back home, during our first telephone conversation, you asked me, "Will the Irish in Ireland work?" You said they were excellent workers in other lands, but you were not so sure of them over here. May I ask if the question still interests you, sir?'

Mr McDonough nodded.

'It's an important question,' he said, 'because if you pay a man 50 cent an hour and he's not a worker, he may actually be costing you $2 or $3 an hour.'

'I can understand that,' I said 'But I don't think it would be wise to ask your question indiscriminately over here. It might put people's backs up. I would suggest that we start off by visiting some cousins of mine. I think we can get some frank answers from them.'

Mr McDonough said I was the doctor.

I leaned over and spoke to the driver: 'Take the road to Ennis and I'll direct you from there.'

It wasn't long before we had pulled up in front of the home of my

Above: The start of the 'Santry Mile', August 1958.

cousin Michael, whom I had met for the first time in my life during my visit to Ireland with Ronnie Delany. Cousin Michael raises beef cattle and farms 200 acres and keeps in close touch with things.

'You can wait in the car,' I said to Mr McDonough, 'and I'll see if they're up yet.' It was just a little after 8 in the morning.

I opened the gate and started up to the front door. I hadn't gone more than a few steps when I was suddenly set upon by two huge dogs who came racing around the side of the house and almost knocked me down and then started nipping and snapping at my wash-and-wear suit as I fought my way to the door.

'Down, boys, down!' I cried, but that only seemed to anger them.

Mr McDonough watched from the car with a bemused look on his face, and I became almost as embarrassed as I was frightened out of my wits.

Then, providentially, there popped into my mind a Gaelic phrase I had heard James Cagney, the actor, use in telling a story one time. Whirling on the dogs I flung out both arms and shouted: '*Fag an bealach!*'

Whether it was the Gaelic command or the waving of my arms that did it, I do not know. But the dogs fell back as if I had thrown scalding water upon, them.

The commotion brought Cousin Michael, a tall, spare man in his fifties, to the front door. He was thunderstruck upon seeing me, but recovered quickly and beckoned to Mr McDonough to come into the house. I ran back to the car to get a brown paper envelope out of my bag. It contained something I had been studying at odd times ever since I went to West Virginia to meet Mr McDonough for the first time: the fat catalogue of the O. Ames Company, the largest shovel factory in the world, now a division of the Bernard P. McDonough Company.

In a little while we were talking away at a great rate over the tea and brown bread that Cousin Michael's wife, Cousin Lena, had served us. When I sensed that the cordiality of the occasion had reached a proper level, I said to Cousin Michael: 'Cousin Michael, Mr McDonough has a question to ask you. I have advised him that it is not a question to be asked of just anyone. I also told him I was sure you would receive it in the proper spirit and not get your back up.'

Cousin Michael and Cousin Lena exchanged glances.

I signalled Mr McDonough like a director giving an actor a cue.

Mr McDonough put down his teacup. He looked from Cousin Lena to Cousin Michael and then he said: 'Will the Irish in Ireland work?'

Suddenly, like the wail of a banshee, there came a great howling, and yowling from the dogs outside the house. It was sheer coincidence, of course. Cousin Michael, however, seemed to welcome the chance to rush to the window and draw aside the curtains and peer out. He turned to Cousin Lena.

'They've a driver out there,' he said. 'Has anyone asked him to have a cup of tea?'

'In a minute,' said Cousin Lena. 'You've been asked a question.'

Cousin Michael came back and sat down in his chair and held his hands out to the electric heater on the floor. Finally, he leaned forward and, looking directly at Mr McDonough, he said:

'They'll work for a stranger.'

Nobody said anything.

'Put a stranger in charge,' said Cousin Michael, 'and he'll make them work. They won't work for anyone they know.'

Mr McDonough pulled out paper and pencil and started making notes. I reached into my brown paper envelope and drew out the shovel factory catalogue. I turned to the page containing the aerial views of the factory, which looked like it might be a branch of General Motors. I handed it to Cousin Michael and said, 'This is Mr McDonough's shovel factory in the United States.'

Cousin Michael took the catalogue carelessly and said again to Mr McDonough: 'They'll work for a stranger. That's the key to the situation.'

Than he looked down at the photograph of the shovel factory. His eyes widened and his mouth fell open a little. He slapped the catalogue smartly and jumped to his feet, 'Put me in charge, Mr McDonough,' he exclaimed. 'I'll make them work!'

There was silence for half a minute and then Cousin Michael realised he had eliminated himself by his previous remarks, and there was a good laugh all around. Cousin Michael asked did we want whiskey or sherry and we said neither this early in the day. Before we got up to leave, Cousin Lena told us that some German industrialists were starting a factory in County Clare (it was the Germans who built the electric power plant on the Shannon years ago) and Mr McDonough raised his eyebrows and made a note of that significant piece of news.

Finally, off we went to visit other County Clare cousins. We missed Cousin Thomas who was off in the bog, too far to fetch. Cousin Johnny was out, and the cousin who has the pub, one of the McDermotts, had not opened up yet. But we found Cousin Delia at home and she sent the boy out into the fields to tell Cousin Paddy.

A TRIBUTE TO THE SHOVEL

Over more tea and brown bread, we talked of enterprises that might be started up in Ireland. Cousin Paddy (he went to agricultural school) said an experimental farm would do the country immeasurable good and Cousin Delia said a sportsman's lodge on the shores of beautiful Lough Derg (a widening of the Shannon, really, and heaven for trout fishermen) would certainly be a sound investment. Mr McDonough nodded in agreement and made notes.

With that we said goodbye and pushed on toward Galway. Along the way, as we passed through a village, Mr McDonough suddenly cried out; 'Pull over to the kerb!'

He was out of the car in a flash, and I followed him and saw what had caught his eye: some shovels on display outside a kind of general store. As Mr McDonough picked one up and examined it, the proprietor came out of the store and introduced himself as Paddy Corcoran.

'I've never seen a shovel like this,' said Mr McDonough.

'That's for cutting turf,' said Mr Corcoran, 'or peat, as you would say, I suppose.'

I ran back to the car and got my brown paper envelope with the shovel catalogue in it. Dashing back, I showed the picture of the big plant to Mr Corcoran.

'This is the largest shovel factory in the world,' I said. 'They turn out 10,000 a day.' I pointed to Mr McDonough, indicating he was the proprietor.

'Go way', whispered Mr Corcoran, looking at the picture. 'Go way–'

'Mr Corcoran,' I said, laughing a little bit in self-deprecation, 'I'll confess something to you. A few weeks ago, I was under the impression that the shovel had gone out of existence in this modern age of machines.'

Mr Corcoran looked at me pityingly,

'My dear man,' he said, speaking as one would to a child, 'the shovel will never go out of existence. I don't care what scientific advances there may be.'

'I believe that now,' I said, 'We'll always need the shovel.'

'The shovel,' said Mr Corcoran, 'is the grandest implement known to civilised man.' He looked at Mr McDonough; who nodded in agreement.

Mr Corcoran turned back to me.

'Just consider now, mister,' he said, 'the shovel is with you all your life. Here in a country such as ours, isn't it the shovel that turns the sod so that seeds may be put down, and the vegetables grown and the oats and barley and all to provide sustenance for the growing child?'

'Yes,' I said, 'that's true, Mr Corcoran.'

Right: A restful moment when training on a deserted Pacific coast beach 40 miles south of San Francisco, 1960.

'Take a lad reaching the threshold of young manhood,' said Mr Corcoran, beginning to warm up to his theme. 'He goes out to look for work. He's untrained. So the prospective employer says to him, "What can you do, m'boy, what can you do?"'

Mr Corcoran looked from one of us to the other, 'Well, now,' he said, 'if the boy can say nothing else, he can certainly say, "I can shovel!" And then, and then what is the employer to reply except, "Well, my lad, that's something, that's something surely. There's a lot of shoveling to be done."'

Mr Corcoran laid a finger alongside his nose. He seemed at a loss for a way to develop his thesis further.

Then across the street, a priest in his cassock walked slowly by, hands clasped behind him, eyes on the walk before him, obviously deep in thought as though he might be pondering next Sunday's sermon.

It was the inspiration Mr Corcoran needed. He thrust out an arm to point.

'Take him,' he whispered. 'Did you ever stop to think, mister, what's waiting for all of us at the end of the road, at the end of the line? Isn't it the shovel in the hands of that holy man as he sprinkles a few clods over the box and speaks in the Latin tongue the words, "Dust thou art, to dust returnest", and down you go and the shovel covers you over?'

Mr Corcoran bent down in a half crouch and spread out his hands.

'Isn't it something to think about, mister?' he croaked. 'Isn't it something to conjure with?'

Mr McDonough put the shovel he was holding back into the rack.

Mr Corcoran straightened up and spoke more rapidly as he saw we were getting ready to move on.

'You talk about your scientific discoveries,' he said, 'your machine age, your atom bomb, your haitch bomb. Have all the scientists, so called, found anything yet that does as much good, that is with a man in life and in death like the shovel?'

Mr McDonough nodded and put out his hand.

'It's been a pleasure to meet you, Mr Corcoran,' he said, 'And you've certainly given us something to think about.'

'Ah, they were just a few thoughts at random,' said Mr Corcoran.

'You'll come inside and have a little drop of something surely?'

'Thank you,' said Mr McDonough, 'but we're behind schedule now.'

At Galway, we went directly (and incognito) to the shovel factory, which turned out to be a foundry really and made other things besides shovels. On a good day, a dozen or so shovels might be produced. The factory had a dirt floor and there were great leather straps turning the machinery. The power came from a generator which was turned by the river flowing underneath the plant. Thinking of the vast shovel factory in West Virginia, I looked at Mr McDonough. He gave no sign of what his reactions were, beyond pulling the sheaf of papers from his pocket and jotting down some notes.

We stopped at the Shamrock Lodge in Athlone for dinner, and while we were eating, the proprietor, Mr Frank Coen, joined us.

'May I ask, gentlemen,' he said politely, 'when ye arrived?'

We said we had landed at Shannon that morning.

'And how long will ye be in Ireland?' We said we thought we would be ready to start back on Monday evening.

A VERY WORTHY CAUSE

Mr Coen looked from one of us to the other and finally he said, in the kindest way: 'Ye arrive on Friday and ye go home on Monday? Ye are stark mad. Why, I went to see a man across the street one Saturday night and we got talking and I didn't come back until Tuesday.'

Next morning, as we rode along the road to Dublin, Mr McDonough referred to the shovel factory for the first time.

'As you can imagine,' he said, 'it would be far more practical for my purposes to build a new factory than to take over the one in Galway.'

'I should think,' I said, 'that the government man we're to meet in Dublin will have some valuable thoughts on that subject.'

'Possibly so,' said Mr McDonough, 'possibly so.' He lit a fresh Sweet Afton cigarette from the butt of another one. He had succeeded in quitting smoking back home, but now he was chain-smoking again, having tired of refusing the cigarettes that were pressed on us every time we met someone new.

I looked out the car window, thinking not of shovels in mass production, but of one particular shovel. This was the one I had arranged with James Cahill of TWA to fly over to Ireland when, and if, I gave the word. We drove past a caravan of tinkers and ancient stone walls with such sentiments painted on them as 'Boycott *An Tostall*' (the annual festival to welcome tourists) and 'Shun Cycling Slaves' the latter a reference to bicycle racers of whatever athletic faction the sign writer happened to be against.

I decided to take Mr McDonough into my confidence.

'Mr McDonough,' I said, 'would you like to hear about a very worthy cause here in Ireland?'

'All right,' he said.

'By way of preface,' I said, 'let me say that since you proposed this weekend visit to Ireland, I have been trying to think of some way to make it sort of symbolic of Irish-American interest in the Old Country.'

'Well,' said Mr McDonough, 'I'll tell you something. I've felt for a long time that the Irish have gone out all over the world and a great many of them have done very well. But I've heard of very few coming back to help Ireland.'

We looked out over the countryside, lush and green, with the fine-looking cattle grazing in the fields.

'This thing I have in mind,' I said after a minute, 'is a campaign to build Ireland's first cinder running track of Olympic standards. Did you know that the country which has produced one of the greatest runners of the mile in Ronnie Delany hasn't a cinder track of her own?'

'If they can produce runners like Delany', said Mr McDonough, 'what do they want with a cinder track?'

'That's just it,' I said. 'Delany left Ireland and went to Villanova University in the United States. They have every facility, including cinder tracks. If he hadn't gone to Villanova, if he had stayed here and been forced to race and train on grass alone, maybe he would never have run a sub-four-minute mile. Ronnie has said as much himself.'

'It seems to me,' said Mr McDonough, 'that Ireland has more pressing problems than cinder tracks.'

'Just a minute', I said. 'Do you admit, sir, that young people are leaving Ireland in great numbers?'

'So I'm told,' said Mr McDonough.

'All right', I went on, 'now consider this. Suppose Ireland was to get her cinder track and start turning out topflight athletes by the dozen. Ronnie himself has said that's possible. Don't you see, sir, the effect on the morale of the youth? Don't you foresee the upsurge in national pride? Don't you see an Irish Olympic team at Rome in 1960 that will be the wonder of the world?'

Mr McDonough lit another Sweet Afton.

'What,' he said, 'is being done to get the cinder track?'

'There's a man in Dublin named Billy Morton', I said. 'He's the big organiser of amateur athletic events and is the honorary secretary of the Clonliffe Harriers.'

'Harriers are hounds, aren't they?' said Mr McDonough.

'Literally speaking, yes', I said, 'But in this sense they are cross-country runners. There are all sorts of running clubs in Ireland, Delany's club is called The Crusaders.'

'There seems,' said Mr McDonough, 'to be an awful lot of running in Ireland.'

'Well,' I said, 'money isn't too plentiful, as you know, and it costs nothing to run. But getting back to Billy Morton, he's got the land for this cinder track at Santry Court on the road to the Dublin airport. Ron Delany is behind him 100 per cent and Mr Briscoe, the Lord Mayor, kicked off the campaign, with a personal donation of £25. That will show you the calibre of people interested in this thing.'

Mr McDonough nodded. 'I'd like to get in on it in a small way,' he said.

'Good,' I said. 'I'll give Billy Morton a ring after we've lunched with the government man.'

The government man (who had been forewarned by Mr Francis W. H. Adams, the former New York police commissioner, that we were on our way) called promptly after we had checked into the Gresham Hotel in Dublin. He turned out to be John Donovan of the Irish Industrial Authority, young and pleasantly owlish-looking, and we went to the men's grill for lunch.

Mr Donovan was full of facts and figures, and there was not a question Mr McDonough put to him about the country that he could not answer out of his head.

Over tea, Mr Donovan said: 'We're getting a great many inquiries from people interested in starting up enterprises in Ireland, but many of them have capital and nothing else. What I mean to say is, they wouldn't know how to conduct a manufacturing business if they started one. Frankly, we're not interested merely in people with money to invest, however laudable their motives may be.'

'You want know-how,' said Mr McDonough.

'Exactly,' said Mr Donovan.

I reached down and brought my brown paper envelope up from under my chair. This time I drew out not only the shovel factory catalogue, but a number of other pieces of literature describing the summer and kitchen furniture and some of the other things that Mr McDonough manufactures. For good measure, I threw in a brochure of the Parkersburg Rig and Reel Company, manufacturers of oil-well drilling equipment. The brochure had a picture of Mr McDonough in it, identifying him as president.

Mr Donovan hastily leafed through the material, leaned back and slapped the table.

'Mr McDonough,' he said, 'you're the kind of man we're looking for. We can make you a very interesting offer which might include the building of a factory, without cost to you, and certain tax exemptions which would have to be worked out.'

They spoke the same language and soon were discussing not only the making of shovels, but the starting up of a toy factory (Ireland would dearly love a toy factory, said Mr Donovan) and the building of light ships and furniture and all sorts of things. There was, of course, no mention of my own heart's desire: a cinder running track for Dublin.

The luncheon ended with Mr Donovan promising to airmail a full report to Mr McDonough and Mr McDonough pledging that after he had studied it, he would send a technical expert to Ireland to go into the matter in detail.

Back in our rooms upstairs, I picked up the telephone and called Billy Morton.

In a moment, Mrs Morton was on the wire, and I told her who I was. We had met last December.

'Ah, what a pity,' exclaimed Mrs Morton. 'Billy will be terribly sorry he missed you. He's in London to sign up Brian Hewson (the four-minute miler) to run against Delany at Lansdowne Road later this month.'

I asked her to hold the wire.

'Bad news!' I said to Mr McDonough. 'Billy Morton is in London.'

Mr McDonough puffed on his cigarette, thinking.

'We could go back home by way of London,' he said. 'It's only about an hour and a half from here by air.'

'Mrs Morton,' I said into the phone, 'we'll fly to London to find Billy. Where will we find him?'

'Just like that, you'll fly to London,' exclaimed Mrs Morton, 'Isn't that grand! Well, you'll find Billy at the Lancaster Gate Hotel. Look sharp now or you may not recognise him. He's had his hair cut.'

'He doesn't wear the hair long any more?'

'No, and I've been after him for years to have it cut short. Do you know what he'd say?'

'No,' I said, 'what?'

'He'd say, "How can I cut my hair short when I'm to conduct the symphony this Wednesday evening?"'

'Ha,' I said, 'that's Billy all right. Very well, Mrs Morton, we're on our way.'

THE LONG AND SHORT OF IT

Two hours later we had checked in at the Dorchester and were sitting in the lounge waiting for Billy to come over from the Lancaster Gate. Soon – short, stocky and breathless – he came bustling in.

I introduced Mr McDonough and than said to Billy: 'Billy, you look years younger with your hair cut short.'

'Do I now,' said Billy, pleased as punch. 'Tell me, boys, what would you take me for?'

'I'd say fifty,' I said.

Billy's face fell,

'Oh, dear God in heaven,' he gasped, 'I'm only forty-seven!'

'Will you let me finish, Billy?' I said. 'What I meant was, I'd say fifty with your hair long, no more than forty with your hair cut short as it is now.'

Billy was only half convinced, but he perked up when I asked him if he had signed Brian Hewson to run against Ron Delany in Dublin later in the month.

'I did,' said Billy, 'and it will be a great event. You know Hewson beat Delany in one race last summer and ran a photo finish in the other, Delany will be out to beat him this time with nothing left in doubt about it at all.'

'And how is your cinder track fund going?' said Mr McDonough.

'Well, sir,' said Billy, 'I'll tell you, Mr McDonough. It's slow work. But the money is coming in little by little and we'll make it eventually. Part of the proceeds of the Delany-Hewson race will go to the fund, of course.'

'Do you think,' said Mr McDonough, 'Ronnie Delany would have become the Olympic champion if he had stayed in Ireland and trained on grass alone?'

'It's a moot question, sir,' said Billy. 'Some people in Dublin say Ronnie is such a natural that he would have won anyway. Others contend that he wouldn't have developed so well without the big-time facilities he enjoyed at Villanova University, to say nothing of the fine coach he has over there.'

'Jumbo Elliott,' I said.

Billy nodded.

'Do you think, Billy,' said Mr McDonough, 'that you'll develop some other fine athletes like Ronnie when you get your cinder track?'

Billy looked around the room and then leaned across the table.

'I prefer to quote Delany himself on that subject,' said Billy. 'Delany said at our first meeting in the cinder track campaign that he would hazard the guess that there are dozens of Irish lads who would be as good, as himself or Eamon Kinsella, the hurdler, if they just had the facilities to train.'

'What a great team Ireland could have in the Olympics at Rome in 1960,' I said.

'That's what I'm saying,' said Billy.

Mr McDonough had reached for his chequebook and, as he wrote, Billy and I glanced airily around the lounge, so as not to watch.

'Here you are, Billy,' said Mr McDonough. 'I'd like to have a little part in the cinder track.'

'Well, thank you, sir,' said Billy, taking the cheque and looking at it. His eyes popped.

Above: Albie Thomas (Australia) leads the field through the first lap in the 'Santry Mile', 6 August 1958.

'A thousand dollars!' he exclaimed. 'Why, this is the largest single donation so far. Thank you, Mr McDonough, not only on my own behalf but on behalf of the thousands of Irish lads who will enjoy the benefits of the cinder track. And let me say, sir, that this is more than a mere donation to the fund. It is proof positive that the sons of Irishmen in America have not forgotten the Old Country and will not stand idly by while she is in need. With your permission, Mr McDonough, I'll announce this grand gift at the ground-breaking by Ron Delany and the Lord Mayor next Wednesday.'

(This was better news than I had dared to hope for; I was counting on a groundbreaking, but I thought it might be months away.)

Mr McDonough shook his head. 'I don't want anything like that, Billy.'

'Ah, it will be a shot in the arm to the campaign, sir,' said Billy. 'You just leave it to me.'

'Tell me, Billy,' I said, reaching under my chair for my brown paper envelope, 'do you have a shovel for the ground-breaking?'

'Well,' said Billy, 'no particular shovel, no. But that's a detail. I'll get one.'

'Take a look at this,' I said, holding out the shovel factory catalogue. 'These are the famous Ames shovels from Mr McDonough's factory.'

'Ah, they're grand shovels,' said Billy, looking at the pictures.

'Let me tell you about them,' I said. 'The Ames shovel is the great American shovel. The first one was made back in 1774, two years before the Declaration of Independence.'

'Yes, yes?' said Billy.

'Now just consider, Billy,' I went on, 'all the historic events in which the Ames shovel must have played a part. The California Gold Rush of '49, the building of the railroads, the breaking of ground for the skyscrapers of New York. You know, of course, that Abraham Lincoln used to do his sums on the back of a shovel, lying before the fire.'

'I believe that is so,' said Billy.

'Chances are', I said, 'Lincoln's shovel was an Ames shovel.'

'Hold on, hold on,' said Billy. 'Maybe I see what you're driving at. Wouldn't it be a grand thing if this historic American shovel could be used to break ground for the cinder track next Wednesday?'

'Well, wouldn't it be a symbol?' I said, 'a shining symbol of the bond between Free Ireland and America?'

'And what could be more fitting,' cried Billy, 'especially since Ronnie Delany will be taking part? A Dublin boy going to school in America puts his boot to a great American shovel to break ground for Ireland's first real cinder track!'

I turned to Mr McDonough,

'Mr McDonough,' I said, 'I had something like this in mind when I left New York, I arranged with Mr James Cahill of TWA to fly a shovel to Ireland on short notice. Could you have a special shovel flown to Idlewild right away? If so, TWA will take it from there.'

Mr McDonough thought a minute.

'I don't see why not,' he said. 'In fact, I believe I could have a special shovel chromium-plated.' He got to his feet.

'I'll call my office right now,' he said. Billy Morton stood up. 'Before you go, sir,' he said, 'may I propose a toast?'

I got up and we all raised our glasses. 'To the great American shovel,' said Billy Morton. 'Let it be borne like an Olympic torch across the sea to Ireland!'

* * *

Things worked out as if they were surely meant to be. Mr McDonough called the shovel factory from London and ordered a beautiful chromium shovel flown to Idlewild.

At Idlewild, 45 minutes after getting word from me to activate our shovel plan, James Cahill of TWA handed the shovel to Capt. William B. Schumacher on Flight No. 992. At Shannon, TWA Agent Finian Fielding put it on an Aer Lingus plane for Dublin, where Patrick Condon was waiting to rush the shovel to the Lord Mayor's Mansion. And there it stayed until the evening of the groundbreaking ceremonies. For that happy occasion, Ronnie Delany (just home from Villanova) and the Lord Mayor (still Robert Briscoe then) put their boots to the shovel while a fine crowd, including every child (said Billy Morton) for twelve miles around, cheered and some of Billy's invited guests raised their glasses in the temporary clubhouse on the cinder track site.

'I was happy,' said Mr Briscoe, 'to be one of the first small subscribers to this project and now I want to give a second subscription equal to what I gave last time.'

Ronnie Delany said that he himself hoped to be able to contribute to the fund before the track and the stadium to go with it were completed. He said he was sure there would be many world records set on the track.

The papers were full of the news of the groundbreaking and the shovel from America, and when Delany ran against Hewson (beating him in the slow time of 4:09.7 – and what would you expect on grass?), 33,000 spectators were on hand at the Lansdowne Road Stadium. Gross receipts were $12,000, a great boost for the cinder track fund. A few days later Billy Morton announced that the Clonliffe Harriers would sponsor a special athletic event each year from now on. It will be a mile run in Dublin and on the new cinder track when it is ready.

There will be a perpetual trophy put into competition. No one will ever win permanent possession of it. But the names of all the winners will be inscribed upon it.

And what do you think this perpetual trophy will be, this prize that Irish lads will strive for as long as there's a Dublin?

It will be Mr McDonough's magic shovel.

* * *

In 1958, there was a postscript to Gerald Holland's series of stories on Ireland in *Sports Illustrated.*

AH, IT WAS A MAGIC SHOVEL!

Well didn't it break ground for Dublin's first cinder track that's now famous forever?

The most famous running track in all the world this week was the cinder track of Ireland's Santry Stadium, on the road to Dublin Airport. For it was here that Herb Elliott set a new world record of 3.54.5 for the mile and three other milers bettered John Landy's old record of 3.58.

The story of these incredible performances in the same race was so astonishing that it burst out of the sports pages and on to Page One of newspapers here and abroad. For readers of *Sports Illustrated*, it was a very special story, one that they had been following and sharing in since January 1957, when the cinder track at Santry was but a gleam in the eye of Ireland's foremost promoter of athletics, indefatigable, irrepressible Billy Morton.

The story began when Associate Editor Gerald Holland was sent to Ireland in the company of Olympic Champion Ron Delany to report on the homecoming celebration for Ireland's greatest athletics hero. ...

The Delany story aroused the interest of a *Sports Illustrated* subscriber, Bernard P. McDonough, of Parkersburg, West Virginia, proprietor of the O. Ames Company, which has been making shovels since Revolutionary days and is the largest shovel factory in the world. Mr McDonough called Associate Editor Holland, proposed that they fly to Ireland for a weekend and see what might be done to help that economically distressed land – either by starting up a shovel factory or doing something that would be symbolic of Irish American concern for the old country.

It seemed to *Sports Illustrated*'s man that if McDonough and Morton could be exposed to each other something would come of it. Moreover the shovel itself seemed to be a symbol that somehow might fit into the picture. So, before takeoff, Holland asked TWA if the airline would fly an American shovel to Ireland at short notice. Mystified, but co-operative, TWA said it would be glad to.

On a whirlwind weekend tour of Ireland, the sportswriter-industrialist team of Holland and McDonough inspected factories, conferred with government officials, were reluctantly forced to the conclusion that old Ireland had shovels enough. This cleared the field for Billy Morton, and when it was discovered that he was not in Dublin at all, but in London, the Americans flew there. And in the lounge of London's Dorchester Hotel, McDonough was confronted with Morton, and the subject of Ireland's need for a cinder track was squarely faced. McDonough, who had never seen Morton before in his life and had been blissfully unaware of the urgent need for a cinder track, gave Morton a cheque for $1,000 and, at the urging of *Sports Illustrated*'s man, agreed to provide one of the historic Ames shovels for the groundbreaking ceremony. TWA, as promised, flew it over the next day.

Last week, as Mr McDonough read of the magic his shovel had helped to work, he cabled Billy Morton a pledge of $5000 to help finish the stands at Santry Stadium 'in the hope that other Irish-Americans will join me.'

ONCE AN OLYMPIAN, ALWAYS AN OLYMPIAN

The impact on your life of winning a gold medal – of being an Olympic Champion – is immense. Life is never the same again. And if you are from a small country you can multiply the effect a hundredfold. The recognition is overwhelmingly positive. You are introduced everywhere as an Olympic Champion. People are not interested in the event you competed in or the time you ran, though when they learn that you won the classic event – the metric mile – they probably are a little more impressed. Sebastian Coe recently said to me 'The 1,500 metres, it is the greatest Olympic race, isn't it Ronnie?' Who am I to disagree?

being able to run.

Winning 'for Ireland' has its own resonance. The Olympics is about national pride and winning is a shared experience. Every four years a nation's aspirations are for Olympic success across the whole spectrum of different sports. The measure of success is gold, silver or bronze. The ultimate moment is to see your flag raised and hear your national anthem played before the world.

If you are the one to achieve what is deemed almost impossible, you become a public property and this ownership becomes more affectionate as the years go by. The mystique of being the Olympic Champion

The statement that 'winning a gold medal' makes is that you are indisputably the champion of the world. You had one chance on one day and you took it. You are now part of the glorious history of the Olympics. You will live with this forever. The young child will look on in amazement when Daddy says 'see that man, he won a gold medal in the Olympics for Ireland'; the child's amazement is about the credibility of this grey-haired, ageing man even

grows to the point of being greater than the reality. The commercialisation of sport, its universality and endless media analysis has led to the Irish public being more aware of what it takes to win and how competitive the world of sport is. Sport has changed, but the race is still the same. On one day every four years your previous reputation counts for little. You go to the starting line and with a combination of desire, intellect and tactical ability have this one chance to prove you are the best.

You live with being the Olympic Champion every day for the rest of your life. In the immediate short term, if you remain a competitor as I did, it goes with the territory. Every time you step on the starting line you are the target. Every athlete wants to beat you, irrespective of the importance of the race. Yours is a scalp to be taken. But if you are as competitive as I was you are not going to be taken easily!

In your life outside sport and after you have retired the public's constant interest in you may seem intrusive and insatiable. I have not had a particular problem with becoming a 'living legend' in Ireland. To a certain extent, I have viewed myself as a public property, a unique curiosity in a nice sort of way. A huge responsibility remains with you to reflect what is best

about Olympism. There is an image, an expectation in the mind of the person who genuinely asks you about your achievement, about what it was like then, or who congratulates you on your success as if it were yesterday.

The Irish public's interest is a compliment to me and to how the Olympics have impacted on their sporting imagination. The very least I can do is listen and respond appropriately. It is not as if I have an insatiable ego or that I am number one for modesty. I know exactly who and what I am and I am comfortable with myself and my role in Irish sport and the wider Irish society. There seldom, if ever, is intrusiveness and if there is I can manage it.

I feel I have been greatly honoured by the Irish public and by my peers over the years. I have received a fulsome quota of accolades in

Left: Bob Tisdall (far right), Ireland's Olympic gold medallist in the 400-metre hurdles, 1932, with my lovely wife Joan (left) and Jimmy and Anne Murphy at the Los Angeles Games, 1984.

the last fifty years and I am sincerely appreciative. And, unlike when I was competing in endless races, I am not alone. I enjoy the love and support of my wife Joan, and so many others in my caring family to whom I am simply Daddy or Papa. I also have my lifelong friends and tennis-playing pals who occasionally accuse me of a dodgy line call (it is not that I am wrong, it's just that Olympic champions have to have better eyesight than other mere mortals!)

I faced my first crisis as a newly crowned Olympic Champion when I returned to Villanova in early January 1957 following my extraordinary 'homecoming' visit to Dublin for Christmas. Villanova University was first and foremost an academic institution. You were expected to attend your classes, take your exams and make your grades. If you were wavering you were firstly made ineligible to compete for the track team and secondly, if you did not improve, to ultimately lose your scholarship. It was not a vain threat. In my freshman year a world-class sprinter from the Caribbean and an American 60-foot shot putter were 'let go', so to speak. If you remained academically ineligible you were of no use to the team.

Through no fault of my own my return flight from Dublin was cancelled and delayed for twenty-four hours. The day I arrived back on campus I was called to the Dean of Disciplines office in Mendel Hall. I was advised that I was not going to be allowed to complete the semester as I had arrived back a day late for classes. This was deemed an abuse of privilege as I had already been given leave of absence to take part in the Olympics. Even though my mid-term grades prior to going to Australia were three As and three Bs, the Dean was not impressed with my argument that I had returned to classes immediately following the Olympics and I was confident I had made up the ground to be able to pass my final exams. He was adamant. I could not complete my exams.

The consequences of this were horrific as far as I was concerned. I would effectively lose six months of my academic life and be unable to graduate with the class of '58. Luckily the Dean allowed me to appeal his decision to the President, Father Donnellan OSA who allowed me, reluctantly I am sure, to return to my classes. I might have been the Olympic hero, but academia was not impressed. I was going to have to complete my studies on their terms, just like any other student. I had learned a sanguine lesson; don't push your luck too far.

On reflection, my approach to studying for my degree was a bit like training for athletics without the same desire or emotional highs and lows. It was a case of simply getting on with it. Listen to your lecturers in class, complete your required papers on time and study with the same regularity as your training on the track. This meant going to the silence and solitude of the library most evenings to study. Besides, my fellow students in my dormitory were a bit like hamsters; they came out to study late at night.

I may have been a scholarship athlete and an Irishman to boot, but by this stage I was beginning to take part in more normal collegiate life. This was one of the most exciting times in American history. It was post-Korean War, the time for chinos, *The Ed Sullivan Show*, 'to see the USA in your Chevrolet', and the emergence of

Above: With Deborah Kerr on the set of Tea and Sympathy *in Hollywood, May 1956, (l-r) Lon Spurrier (US), Bill Dillinger (US) and Jim Bailey (Australia).*

the King, Elvis Presley. If anything was a symbol of the original rock and roll generation it was the Chevy with its chromed 'V' on the bonnet front, two-colour paint scheme and fins framing the boot. If anyone tested the norms of American conservatism it was Elvis and his gyrations on TV.

One smart decision I made was not to room with another athlete. I chose a student friend interested primarily in studying towards his degree. It was an added bonus if his interests extended to extra-curricular activity. One of my roommates was Ken Gerg, a second-generation German from St Mary's, Pennsylvania. He was a hunter and he might have been an athlete if he

had been at any other university. We are friends to this day. He was a millionaire by the time he was fifty, retired and sold his business and concentrated his time since then on the triathlon. Another roommate was John La Croix from Rye, New York where he still lives. He became USA Vice-President of Saatchi & Saatchi in New York. Probably the brightest student I knew.

Pat Nicholson from Toledo, Ohio and I shared

a room in the newly-built Sheehan Hall on campus. Pat was class president and persuaded me to run for class treasurer in my junior year. I stood for election – or should I say ran – in May '56 and was the first and only candidate to use national television as part of his campaign strategy. My mile race in the Los Angeles Coliseum against John Landy was televised live across the United States on the same day as the Kentucky Derby. I won the election, but not the race! Pat ended up owning Nicholson Concrete in Ohio and establishing N-VIRO Energy, which he continues to promote.

A privilege of having close friends and team-mates at Villanova was being invited to their homes up and down the East Coast. At Al Ligorelli's house in West Philadelphia I was to experience Italian cuisine worthy of the best restaurants in Naples or Rome. The Gerg family in upstate Pennsylvania were not to be outdone and the wienerschnitzel Ken's mother prepared could rival the best in the world! I witnessed American family life at its best and could not fail to be impressed.

I also enjoyed many pleasant visits to the homes of American girls I dated. I had one problem though; being an athlete, I had a voracious appetite. I sometimes thought it was prudent to eat dinner at the college before inflicting myself upon some unsuspecting American mother! And as I ate helping after helping the lovely mother might remark, 'Haven't you a wonderful

appetite! It's a pleasure to feed you.'

I did involve myself in extra-curricular activity where time allowed. I was a member of Opera Classical, a musical appreciation society, the Turf and Tinsel Club, which put on theatrical revues, and the Varsity Club as well as being my class treasurer. I also played Colonel Pickering in G.B. Shaw's *Pygmalion*, put on at the nearby girls' school, Rosemont College. One thespian remarked when critically assessing my performance – 'as an actor you are an excellent runner, Ronnie.'

I also attended the Junior Prom, the jazz concert, the Homecoming Ball and any other event of note on the Villanova social calendar, as well as the fun events in the local girls colleges, Rosemont, Immaculata and Bryn Mawr. I really enjoyed the friendship, the company and the affection of the girlfriends I dated in my student years at Villanova. I can only look back fondly on a very special time in my life when I was almost the 'All-American Boy' for at least nine months of the year.

Opposite page: An evening at home with the Bowden family in San José, California in 1960 – no doubt watching The Ed Sullivan Show.

This page: These photos relate to my less than brilliant acting career in G.B Shaw's Pygmalion *and Lady Gregory's* The Rising of the Moon.

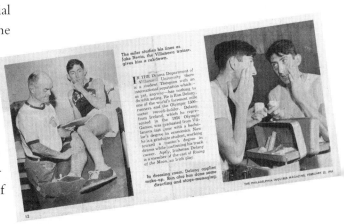

145

But in my heart I yearned for life as I knew it in Ireland. I would take the first available flight home to Dublin when I had fulfilled my commitments to the track team, usually racing in the National Collegiate Championships wherever they were being held, in say Berkeley, California or Austin, Texas.

The theory of being home in Ireland for the summer was that I was, quote, 'on holidays'. On the one hand I had an incredible time enjoying the lifestyle of Ireland and Dublin, in particular, with the emphasis on having a ball with my lifelong friends. We partied, we danced our feet off at tennis club hops, went to the cinema and theatre and enjoyed any good spells of weather we

got. On the other hand, I really had to run a lot of races in Dublin and Europe each summer when I was home. The delightful athletics promoter at that time, the late Billy Morton of Clonliffe Harriers, saw to that.

I would hardly have landed at Shannon when he would have me racing against the best in Britain, Europe and elsewhere in a packed College Park, Santry Stadium or Lansdowne Road. I also had to accept invitations abroad and compete in various championships representing Ireland at the behest of the Irish Athletic Association. I was able to accommodate it all for I had a sense of responsibility to the Irish sporting public. Besides I loved to run, to race and

Left: The Villanova track team set out for Austin, Texas to win the NCAA Championship, June 1957; in front Ed Collymore, Ronnie Delany, Coach Elliott, Alex Breckenridge and Charlie Jenkins, with Phil Reavis, Charles Stead and Don Bragg to rear.

hopefully to win. It was not ideal for me, but I was prepared to take up the challenge.

The long cross-country, indoor and outdoor seasons in America from September through June did not count for much to the expectant Irish fan who was perhaps seeing me run for the first time. It did not really matter that I might have raced in America at least twenty times earlier that year. The irony of it was that the pundits around that time used to write about the American system burning out the talent that was Ronnie Delany. If there was to be any doubt about it, the Irish athletic promoters seemed hellbent on trying to prove them right.

The foregoing is not an excuse for the occasional defeat I suffered during the summer months when home from America. It is not a plea some fifty years later for a little sympathy and more understanding. I faced up to every challenge presented to me. When I suffered a defeat my opponent had better watch out, as I usually resolved to beat him the second time round. My win/loss record clearly shows this.

I always learned more from defeat than from victory and was able to rationalise the reasons why, whether in America or elsewhere. Looking back, my worst performances on record were at times when I was tactically naïve or when I was carrying an injury. The latter was the most difficult to manage. Recurring injuries to my Achilles tendon were to lead to my early retirement from athletics in 1962. My swansong was

appropriately enough to be in New York's Madison Square Garden in March, running the fourth leg on an Irish relay team that finished second to a crack Canadian team anchored by the on-form Bill Crothers. I was not accustomed to losing in the Garden.

The following citation written by Stan Saplin of the *New York Post* some thirty years later best encapsulates what I mean:

'Nobody has had an indoor mile career to match that of Ronald Michael Delany, who came to Villanova as a 19-year-old freshman in 1954.

'From January 1956, as a Wildcat sophomore, through March of 1959 when he retired, Delany ran 34 major indoor mile races against all kinds of foes, domestic and foreign, and he won them all.

'What's more, nobody ever threatened him. He ran leisurely and enjoyable, happy to win, just as a latter day Irishman from Villanova named Eamonn Coughlan also seemed to relish his victories. Whereas Eamonn, however, made serious efforts to break world records, which he did in the indoor mile three times, Delany also broke the indoor world record for the mile three times, without trying to do so. In fact, prior to his first record-breaking mile during his senior year. Ron's indifference to the clock sometimes infuriated fans and he heard boos on occasion, merely because he chose simply to win.

'He first brought the record down to 4:03.4.

Then in a two week span he lowered it to 4:02.5 and finally to 4:01.4. Had Ron stayed with the sport, undoubtedly he would have been the first to run a sub-four mile indoors. Instead that distinction went to Jim Beatty, who erased Delany's WR with 3:58.9 effort in Los Angeles in 1962.

'Delany's mile streak might have been 36, rather than 34. But twice, to help Villanova pick up needed points in the IC4A championships, he passed up the mile and ran both the two-mile and the 1,000 – 48 minutes apart – and both times won them both.

'Don't assume Ron Delany was just an indoor runner; in 1956 he merely won the Olympic 1,500-metre crown, trouncing an incredibly fast field of international stars in an Olympic record

Above: Olympic Champions reunion: with Herb Elliott (Australia) and Peter Snell (New Zealand) in Sydney, 25 November 1977, for a This Is Your Life programme on Herb Elliott.

time of 3:41.2. He bettered four minutes three times during his career, with his best time 3:57.5. And if this sounds less than consequential to present day fans, remember this was more than thirty years ago when Delany beat four minutes for the first time, he was only the seventh man ever to do so.'

In the history of indoor athletics in America it is remarkable that Eamonn and I, two Irish runners from the same university, should have dominated the scene so dramatically. I use the term deliberately for performing indoors to me was like theatre in the round. Picture any smoke filled arena at the time, literally across the United States. Running indoors was much more popular then and every meeting was a sell-out. The track was made of wood with eleven laps to the mile, compared to four laps outside. The bends were tight and sharply sloped. We ran in shoes with minute spikes and the boards actually splintered.

The excitement of the race was enhanced for the spectator by the multi-laps, the tight bends and the short straightway. Running indoors required far greater tactical skill, the ability to negotiate the bends and an explosive finish. The spectators watching the race from close up for the premium seating framed the perimeter of the track, right up to the rooftop. I remember the scene

so vividly – the officials in their tuxedos and the ladies in their minks and diamonds cheering and clapping, and if that was not enough a mini-orchestra or band played in tempo with the beat of the running feet. 'Flight of the Bumblebee' was appropriate to the 60-yard dash or high-hurdles. A popular Strauss waltz best suited the mile race. I never listened to the music during my races, but I am given to understand that 'When Irish Eyes are Smiling' was a popular number when I was amassing my unbeaten streak.

There was an intimacy about running indoors, of being so close to the spectators that brought out the performer in you. I ran to win and Eamonn raced the clock, becoming the first man ever to run a sub-3:50 mile indoors. We were the stars of the show and the thespian in each of us meant that we entertained our audience like acting veterans from the Abbey or the Gate Theatre back in Dublin. This tradition was carried on by a litany of great Irish middle distance runners throughout the past millennium, none less than world champions Marcus O'Sullivan and Frank O'Meara.

The commercialisation of sport and the high payments sought by the athletes unfortunately brought about the demise of indoor athletics in America. Another factor was the building of larger arenas that could accommodate a

STUDY IN GREEN—Ron Delany, Ireland's gift to Villanova's track prominence in the indoor one-mile run, receives congratulations on his victory in the Wanamaker Mile during the Millrose Games in Madison Square Garden from Dr. Shane MacCarthy, Executive Director of the President's Council on Youth Fitness. Dan Ferris, Honorary Secretary of the A.A.U., observes the greeting after making the introduction

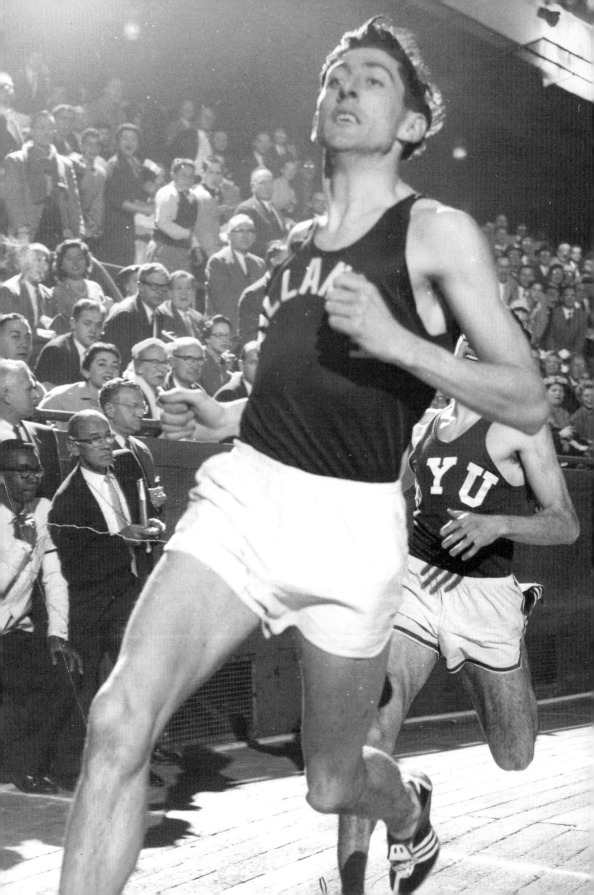

Left: Winning the 1,000 yards in the IC4A Championship, Madison Square Gardens, 2 March 1957 against Ike Matza (NYU). This was the first leg of my unprecedented 1,000 yard / two mile double in the championship, which I was to repeat in 1958.

200-metre synthetic track negating the excitement of the boards as I experienced it. On the East Coast up to recently only one meet remained, the Millrose Games in the new Madison Square Garden in New York, where Eamonn and I repeatedly won the famed Wannamaker Mile. The *Inquirer* Games in Philadelphia are gone along with Boston, Chicago, Milwaukee, Cleveland and the four other meets held each winter in New York.

I only wish people in Ireland could have seen me running indoors. The Irish media at the time barely covered my unbeaten career. A win merited a few column inches at best. However, I was the lead sports story, week-in, week-out, during the indoor season in the *New York Times, Chicago Daily News, Boston Herald* and so on. The US media made a huge story about my winning streak, stretching as it did over five years. It captured their imagination and appealed to the American sports fan's fixation with batting averages, yards gained or win-loss records. One of my favourite headlines, which appeared in *Sports Illustrated,* ran 'How to Beat Delany. Oops!'

I ran so often indoors that I can't really recall the detail of so many races. My more lasting memories are of when I 'doubled up' for the team and ran the 1,000 yards and two-mile run

to ensure that Villanova won the Intercollegiate (IC4A) Championships in successive years in New York. It never occurred to me at either time that I was putting my winning streak at risk. The joy of sharing in a team victory far outweighed any such consideration.

Another victory I savoured during 1959 was stepping down to the half-mile to take on New York's favourite son, Tom Murphy, in the Garden before a largely hostile crowd. I won lit-

bly one of the most competitive foot races ever seen in New York.

In contrast, the following weekend in the Garden I was cheered to the rafters when I broke my own world record for the indoor mile with a time of 4 minutes 02.5 seconds beating Istvan Rozsavolgyi of Hungary in the process. Istvan made me run even faster one week later, when to beat him I had to set a new world record of 4 minutes 01.4 seconds. I was never

erally by a whisker – or maybe I should say a nose – to extend my winning streak to thirty-four. Such are the vagaries of the sports fan, however, that I was roundly booed after proba-

Above: Eventually getting the better of Tom Murphy in the 880 yards at the NYAC Games, Madison Square Gardens, 14 February 1959 – my thirty-fourth consecutive victory indoors since March 1955.

destined to run an indoor mile in Madison Square Gardens again, so, somewhat ironically for a man who never ran to beat the clock, I went out on a really high note.

I can also clearly recall the gradual build-up of pressure and mental stress related to my successive victories. It was not so much the different athletes I had to compete against each week, but rather the psychological effect of having to continue to win, win, win. I was human and I usually read race previews in the sports pages before I ran. All the talk was about whether I would be beaten that night or extend my winning streak. It was certainly stressful.

I can recall one particular race when my mind began to play strange tricks on me. It was in the first few laps, the pace was slow, and the thought occurred to me that I was sick and tired of having to bust my gut each weekend to win another race. I began to picture a scenario in my own mind of feigning a stitch in my side, stepping off the track and trying to explain to the media afterwards of how I could not have continued to run because of the pain. The subsequent thought that I might be taken to a hospital to explore what was wrong with me brought me quickly back to reality. I quickened my stride and took after the leading runners with a new-found desire to win again. Luckily for me, I suppose, I have hated hospitals and being sick in any way all my life.

The other issue I muse over at times is the latent damage caused to my Achilles tendons by running indoors. I retired, prematurely perhaps, because of damaged tendons. The strain on the tendon must have been immense on the board tracks. Shoe design had not advanced to the

Ron Couldn't 'Gamble' In 880 Victory in N. Y.

NEW YORK, Feb. 15 (UPI).— Track and field fans are strange —they booed Ron Delany for reeling off his 34th straight indoor victory and then cheered themselves hoarse for John Thomas, who high-jumped seven feet for the second time in two weeks.

The Dublin-born Delany made it plain he didn't appreciate the boos which greeted his winning half-mile effort of 1:52.2 in the New York AC Games at Madison Square Garden last night.

He conceded "the finish was a little slow," but complained rather bitterly about "the New York crowds which always boo me" and said he doesn't get that treatment anywhere else.

Delany took just the opposite tack from Ted Williams, of the Red Sox, who says he gets booed in many places, including Boston, but rarely in New York.

UP WITH LEADERS

At any rate, Delany found he couldn't run his own race so much in the half-mile as he usually does in his mile specialty.

"In the mile, I can gamble and lay back," he said. "In the half-mile I have to stay up with the leaders."

Dropping down to the half-mile Saturday night after registering his 28th straight mile triumph in the Philadelphia Inquirer Games Friday night, Delany barely beat Manhattan's Tom Murphy with former Pitt star Arnie Sowell finishing third and England's Mike Rawson fourth.

The crowd derived its biggest kick of the night, however, from Thomas' brilliant leap.

The 17-year-old Boston University freshman became the fifth man in history to clear seven feet in the high jump—and the only one indoors—two weeks ago at the Millrose Games here.

That record was contested because Olympic champion Charley Dumas, only other American to jump seven feet, jumped immediately after Thomas and knocked down the bar before it could be re-measured.

But there was no doubt about Thomas' seven-foot jump last night. He made three passes at 7 feet, 1¼ inches and barely knocked the bar off during the second of his three misses.

stage of minimising impact damage. Medical science or sports medicine was in its infancy.

Running on less than scientifically designed grass tracks, cinders and baked sand prior to the emergence of the tartan or synthetic track must not have been doing my tendons any good over time. I should also take into account the adverse effect of running cross-country each autumn in America. 'Cross-country' was a bit of a misnomer, for most of the courses I ran on during my intercollegiate career were along tarmacadamed public roads and stony pathways. Though I may have retired prematurely from competitive athletics, I have managed to play other sports all my life right up to now, so don't be deterred if you are an aspiring Olympian or fitness fanatic!

THE GREATEST LITTLE TRACK TEAM IN THE WORLD

Sports pundits argue that I reached the peak of my outdoor athletics career in Melbourne. This view is compounded by my failure to make any impact at the Rome Olympics in 1960. What this assessment fails to take into account is my career in intercollegiate athletics competing for Villanova, 'the greatest little track team in the world', as we were called then. We were a small team, but a phenomenally successful one, winning a succession of American Collegiate and Inter-Collegiate titles and Relay Championships of America between 1954 and

1958. Individually, Charles Jenkins, Don Bragg and I consistently won our specialities at invitational meets all over America and in the National Championships wherever they were held.

I peaked repeatedly for Villanova, indoors and outdoors post-Melbourne. I had unprecedented success in the National Collegiate Athletics Championships of America (NCAA) winning a unique mile and half-mile double in 1958 in Berkeley, California. My mile time was 4 minutes 03.5 seconds and I 'repeated' some forty minutes later, winning the half-mile in 1 minute

48.5 seconds. This was the fastest ever double in athletics history and became known thereafter as 'The Delany Double'. A year earlier at the NACA championships in Austin, Texas I had almost brought off the same double winning a tactical mile in a slowish 4 minutes 06.5 seconds and 35 minutes later finishing second in the half-mile in a time of 1 minute 47.8 seconds to my friend Don Bowden of the University of California. Don's winning time was 1 minute 47.2 seconds. My time was a new Irish national record. I sometimes wonder what times I could have run in the half-mile if I had not had to win the mile beforehand as a sort of 'warm up'. I also wonder what my destiny would have been if I had concentrated on the half-mile and had never taken up the mile. And to answer the obvious question in some people's minds – 'No, I could *not* have achieved an 800 metres/1,500

Left: The victorious Villanova track team, 1957.

Above: Relaxing at the soda fountain in the Coast Creamery with Don Bowden, the first American to run a 4-minute mile.

Page 156: Honours ceremony at the 1958 Penn Relays, (l-r) Earl Warren (Chief Justice of the USA), Melbourne Olympic gold medallists Bobby Morrow, Glenn Davis, Gregory Bell and Ron Delany, with Harry Waibel, Gaylord P. Harnwell (President of the University of Pennsylvania) and Thomas Hamilton (Athletic Director, University of Pennsylvania).

Page 157: Defending my half-mile title in the IC4A Championship at the Villanova track, 31 May 1958.

metres double in Melbourne.'

However, one of the most pleasurable doubles I ever achieved was in 1957 at the Meet of Champions in Houston, Texas. I won the mile in 4 minutes 05.4 seconds and after a 45 minutes interval beat my old rival Tom Courtney, the reigning Olympic 800-metre champion, in a time of 1 minute 48.4 seconds. Tom never got the chance to avenge this defeat. It was unusual to have two Olympic gold medallists going head to head in intercollegiate competition, and to be beaten by me after I had won the mile was a bit of an embarrassment to Tom. Of course, there was no malicious intent on my side and

Tom Courtney bears me no ill will, though he's quoted as good-humouredly saying, 'I'll never forgive Delany! Tell him I want a rematch even if it has to be tennis or golf!'

The opportunity to run for Villanova relay teams was infrequent enough over my time there as a student athlete. I mostly ran individual races by invitation only from the meet promoters. Besides, the Villanova team was relatively small in numbers compared to the major universities such as UCLA or Southern California. There was one exception however, namely the Penn Relays held annually in Franklin

Field Philadelphia.

The Penn Relay Championships of America held in April is the oldest relay carnival in America. Confined to high schools and universities, over 5,000 athletes took part in the two-day relay festival. The event attracted up to 50,000 colourful spectators enjoying the spring sunshine. It had no equal in the sporting calendar of Philadelphia and was as much a social as a sporting event, comparable in a way to the RDS Horse Show in Dublin.

I ran for Villanova on ten winning relay teams from 1954 through 1958. The individual prize for the winners was not the usual gold medal, but a much sought after Penn Relays watch supplied by the famous Hamilton Watch Company. There is a story of its own in what I did with so many watches: I presented them to people who were helpful to me in my sport. Charlie Farnham the equipment manager at Villanova who supplied me with clean shorts, running singlets and white socks every day received one with my thanks. Jake Nevin the diminutive tobacco-chewing trainer and masseur deservedly got one for his magical rubs and homespun philosophy that eased the burden of training and the associated muscular pain. It was a nice feeling for me to be able to show a little appreciation.

Relay running gave you the opportunity to

relish the excitement of a team event. I ran for Villanova with an added fervour and pride before my hometown fans and shared that unique friendship, camaraderie, or whatever you want to call it peculiar to team sport. You also had the added responsibility of wanting to win for your teammates and not wanting to let them down.

gold medal. And if this was not enough, his son Chip Jenkins was to win a further gold medal as a panel member on the US 4 x 400 metres relay team at the 1988 Olympics. The expression 'a chip off the old block' comes to mind!

I have described earlier my friendship with Charles in the build up to the Melbourne Games. I mentioned we were alike in so many

My most distinguished and accomplished teammate was undoubtedly Charles Jenkins from Cambridge, Mass. Charlie won the 400-metres Olympic gold in 1956. He also ran the fastest leg on the victorious US 4 x 400 metres relay team in Melbourne, winning his second

ways, driven by ambition and pushing each other in training towards our ultimate goal. Charles Jenkins had a New England elegance about him and subsequently was to enjoy a distinguished career in Washington DC. He was charming and witty and excelled himself on one occasion when visiting me in Dublin. I introduced him to the leading social columnist Terry O'Sullivan of the *Evening Press* at a hastily-convened press conference in the Gresham Hotel. I overheard Terry asking Charlie privately had he even been required to attend lectures as a student in Villanova. Charles's reply to the effect that 'surely Mr O'Sullivan you must have recognised by now that I am a well-educated Villanova Alumnus by the manner in which I have been answering your interesting questions.' Terry O'Sullivan was totally disarmed and reported his conversation with Charles verbatim in his column the following evening.

Charles and I have remained sincere friends even though I chose to return to live permanently in Dublin in 1960. In an in-depth interview during the year 2000 with P.J. Browne, the Irish-born New Jersey-based sports columnist, he said:

'I told him [Ronnie] (at the time) he was crazy. But he kept to his word and I think his time in America strengthened his love for his homeland. He could have pushed the Olympic thing, stayed in America and made himself a fortune. But that wasn't for Ron.'

In the course of the same interview with P.J. Browne, Charlie paid me an extraordinary compliment to this effect:

'No runner has come remotely close to

Opposite left: Ed Moran (Penn State) chases me home as I complete a half-mile/mile double in the IC4A Championships at Villanova – a repeat of my 1957 performance in Randall's Island, New York.

emulating what Delany did when he was at Villanova University. That includes the Irish, the Americans or any nationality you care to mention. For three straight years (1955-1958) he went undefeated indoors running any distance he was asked – the 1,000 yards, the 880, the 1 mile and 2 mile. Bear in mind that the competition he went up against during that time frame was fierce. Delany was competing against Olympic champions almost on a weekly basis and winning. This is a remarkable accomplishment. I don't think he can ever be honoured enough in Ireland for his contribution to athletics. He was truly one of a kind. I feel privileged to know him.'

What can I say, Charlie! I can only say that the pleasure was mine, and thank you for your friendship.

All the members of the ten winning Penn Relay teams I was part of shared equally in the achievement and the joy of being on a victorious team. No one of us could have done it without the others. Our achievements live on in the annals of the relays, the track history of Villanova and with pride in our memories.

I am going to mention the names of some of the Villanova Harriers I ran cross-country with: Johnny Kopil and George Browne, the statutorily-challenged 'pen and pencil' set from Bayonne, New Jersey; Bill Rock and my Scottish friend Alex Breckenridge from Glasgow. We had fun beating West Point and Navy in dual meets along with the local opposition, St Josephs, De La Salle and all others. Alex, who was was American by birth, went on to represent the United States in the marathon at the Rome Olympics in 1960.

Olympic contemporaries of mine at Villanova included Phil Reavis (high jump 1956) and Don 'Tarzan' Bragg who won the gold medal in the pole vault at the Rome Olympics (1960). Don was nicknamed 'Tarzan' because as a teenager he developed his phenomenal upper body strength swinging on ropes from tree to tree in woods near his Jersey home. Don's ambition was to win the

Below: Here we go again – a much depleted Villanova track team about to fly out to the 1958 NCAA Championship in Berkeley California; Phil Reavis (shaking hands) John Buckley, 'Jumbo' Elliott and Ed Collymore.
Right: A smiling finish as Villanova beat the much-fancied Oxford University team in the distance medley at the Penn Relays, Philadelphia, 28 April 1956.

Olympics, of course, and to emulate another American Olympian, Johnny Weismuller, by playing Tarzan in the movies. Incredible though it may seem, Don was actually headhunted to play the role by a producer; they shot the film somewhere in the Caribbean, but it never saw the light of day. There was a copyright dispute with another company who claimed the intellectual property rights to Tarzan and Don's company were injuncted in the US courts from showing the film anywhere.

I don't think Don ever got over his disappointment. Some years later Joan and I met him and his lovely wife when they were visiting Ireland. I collected them at their hotel to go out to dinner and after the usual pleasantries Don asked me how I was 'managing to adjust my ego'. Obviously he was having a problem with his! I just thought the question was hilarious; living in Ireland, having an ego was just not on. Besides, I was never headhunted to play Christy Mahon in *The Playboy of the Western World*. Noel Pearson, where are you?

To wrap up the Villanova connection, I must mention our track coach James 'Jumbo' Elliott. Jumbo earned his nickname at Philadelphia's West Catholic High School, apparently because he was so skinny rather than the opposite. Coach Elliott was an outstanding quarter miler and potential Olympian in the mid-1930s when he retired abruptly from athletics to take up the position of Head Track Coach at Villanova. He was a scratch golfer, was to become a self made multi-millionaire in the construction industry and his own life story, entitled *Maker of Milers, Maker of Men*, was written by his life long friend Dr Ted Berry.

Coach Elliott was an extraordinary motivator and manager of men with athletic talent. He was intuitive and knew from the moment he first saw me run that I would become a miler. This was a remarkable observation to make after watching me run for just a few minutes. Charles Jenkins is reported as saying,

'What you had to understand about Elliott was that he was a very practical kind of person. He recognised talent and had the knack of keeping runners in top physical shape from November to June. He emphasised repeatedly the necessity to rest. "How are you feeling?" he would ask. "Take a couple of days off". But he also had an uncanny sense of when an athlete could produce the big performance.'

I had my own ideas about training and a developing sense of running tactics when I first met Coach Elliott as a nineteen-year-old freshman. I was probably not the most coachable of athletes. I was self-trained and set in my ways. Nonetheless Jumbo was to become the manager of my future athletics career. He took total and complete charge. He told me what workouts I should do (with a degree of consultation), where I was racing and how I should study and look after myself. He was the dominant influence on my athletic career from the day I met him.

Coach Elliott's contribution to my success was huge, but in ways that are often unacknowledged. He knew early on that I had the potential to be an Olympic champion. He recognised that I had the aspiration and the desire, but more than anything else that I had the ability. Elliott believed that on my day I was capable of holding my own with any athlete in the world. What Coach Elliott provided for me was

Above: With the Netherlands' Fanny Blankers (four gold medals, London Olympics 1948) and Ireland's gold medallist hammer-thrower, Dr Pat O'Callaghan (Amsterdam 1928 and Los Angeles 1932).

direction and leadership and that vital intangible – a growing self-confidence. He was without peer as a motivator. He succeeded in instilling in me a winning attitude and the confidence associated with this.

Subsequent to my athletic career Jumbo Elliott established himself as one of the leading middle-distance coaches in the world. Ask the succession of Irish athletes who became American, European and World Champions while under his tutelage. We all recognise the debt of gratitude we owe him for helping us

DIEGES & CLUST
MANUFACTURING
SPECIALTY JEWELERS
NEW YORK · BOSTON
PITTSBURGH · CHICAGO
PROVIDENCE · NEW ORLEANS

achieve our potential. Another measure of the man is the countless Villanovans from America, Europe and Africa that he coached who went on to represent their country in the Olympics with great distinction.

Villanova's win in the NCAA Championship in Austin, Texas in 1957 with a six-man team was truly remarkable then and since. The magnitude of this achievement becomes clear when you realise that universities like USC sent sixty athletes to the finals. Villanova's team victory hinged on my scoring in the mile and half-mile, Jenkins winning the 440 yards and Bragg the pole-vault. Phil Reavis and Alex Breckenridge put icing on the cake by scoring in their specialities. Remarkable yes, but on reflection we were all Olympians with three gold medals already in the bag and with Bragg to add to the collection three years later with his golden vault in Rome.

Bragg, Jenkins and I were gold medallists on the same small track team, attending a relatively unknown Villanova University with a previously unheralded coach. What an extraordinary environment to be training in at Villanova compared to what I had recently left back in Ireland. Written up in large letters on the walls of the changing rooms in the Villanova field house on Lancaster Avenue were the words 'Win or Bust'. This was our mantra. Second place or a fast time was simply not good enough to be a member of this elite team. Coach Elliott was economical with his words of praise and winning became the expected thing.

Almost daily from September through May, in sunshine or freezing cold, Jumbo was alongside the training track, stopwatch in hand, elegantly dressed in his cashmere coat and hat, drilling into us the essentials of running. He put great emphasis on balance and relaxation. He would shout at us 'relax, relax' as we ran around countless circuits of the cinder or board track. This got into your brain to the point where you had a

sense of your legs almost being detached from your body. You were running effortlessly, with maximum economy and without any inward stress or strain. I was not a stylish runner by any description. But in my own mind and body I was poetry in motion in the tradition appropriately of the ancient Greeks and Romans. What I learned from him enabled me to win an Olympic 1,500-metres final and gold medal for Ireland. For that and the many other positive influences he had on my life I remain truly appreciative. Words are totally inadequate to describe my indebtedness to Jumbo Elliott and my Alma Mater, Villanova University.

Opposite left: One of four Championship of America medals I won at the AAU Indoor Championships in Madison Square Gardens between 1956 and 1959.

Above: The Ireland chapter of the Villanova Alumni Association at a gala dinner in Dublin, 26 March 2001: (front row, l-r) Jimmy Reardon, Marcus O'Sullivan, Sonia O'Sullivan, Ronnie Delany, Des McCormack, Fr Dobbin, OSA (President of Villanova University), Eamonn Coughlan, Gary Olsen and (back) Robert Rigsby.

SENSATIONAL RACES

In the period 1957 to 1962 I was to run outdoors representing Ireland in the European Championships (1958), the Rome Olympics (1960) and the World Student Games in Sofia, Bulgaria (1961). I finished second to Derek Ibbotson of Great Britain when he set his new world record of 3 minutes 57.2 seconds for the mile at the White City, London in July 1957. A little over a year later I was racing in Santry Stadium on 6 August against a team from the Antipodes who were hell bent on smashing Ibbotson's record and beating me in the process. This was the night of the famous Santry Mile when Herb Elliott of Australia set an incredible new world standard of 3 minutes 54.5 seconds. I finished third in 3 minutes 57.5 seconds.

In between and around these events I ran an extensive series of match races in Dublin and Europe outdoors, intercollegiate competitions and invitational races in America (indoors and outdoors) as well as featuring on a world class Irish two-mile relay team that set European and other records. However, my racing schedule from mid-1959 until my retirement in early 1962 was curtailed by recurring Achilles tendon injuries. I spite of this, I took part in two world mile record races, won a bronze medal in the European Championships (Ireland's first ever medal at this championship), set new records with the Irish relay team and, finally, won a world title for Ireland in the 800

Above: A gold medal won in the 800 metres at the World University Championships in Sofia, Bulgaria, September 1961.

Opposite: My close friend, and President of Crusaders A.C., Captain Theo Ryan, looks after me again at Lansdowne Road.

metres final at the World Student Games. In retrospect, it wasn't a bad five years!

The White City race was described as the most sensational mile in history – the first four men were inside four minutes and the winner Derek Ibbotson cracked the world record held by John Landy of Australia by eight-tenths of a second with a time of 3 minutes 57.2 seconds. I finished second, Stanislav Jungwirth of Czechoslovakia the 1,500-metres world record holder was third and Ken Wood (Britain) fourth. The race was watched by 30,000 cheering fans and by an estimated television audience of ten million people. Derek was in brilliant form that night and even though there was a suggestion at the time that I was 'boxed in by the Brits' there is no way I could have beaten him. I ran as hard and as well as I could in trying to catch him. The distance between us at the finish was twelve yards.

Ten days later we had a rematch in Dublin on the five laps to the mile grass track at Lansdowne Road before 25,000 partisan fans. There was no question of a world record. But there was a lot at stake in terms of pride, reputation and responsibility on my part to the Irish sporting public.

Before the race Ibbotson, always the cavalier Yorkshireman, shook hands with me and I recall him saying, 'The laddie who wins this race is a good laddie.'

What a race, what a contest of remarkable intensity. With no disrespect to Ibbotson those 25,000 people at Lansdowne Road had not come along to see me beaten! I duly obliged with a blistering sprint from the last bend to surge into the lead and win by a comfortable two yards in 4 minutes 05.4 seconds. It was so exciting to watch that it made my many jousts with Brian Hewson look like kindergarten stuff.

The headline in the *Evening Press* next day ran, 'Delany Regains Mile Crown – and 25,000 Sane People go Mad!' Hats, umbrellas, and newspapers – in fact anything handy – soared into the air. The crowd were deranged, distracted and almost dancing with hysterical delight. It was an unforgettable moment in Irish sport. For in a way I had regained the mythical, or unofficial, world mile championship title that I had lost at White City.

Ibbotson was gracious, as ever, in defeat. He is quoted some years later as humorously saying that Billy Morton ensured that the ground staff at Lansdowne Road did not cut the grass too short so that he wouldn't be able to get away from me!

I never raced a mile on a grass track again, or indeed against Ibbotson. Some years later we played squash against each other in the Fitzwilliam Club. Derek arrived without his racquet so I loaned him my best one. He was the over-forty squash champion of Yorkshire and won the game. However, Lansdowne Road was to be revisited! I arranged a rematch, set him up by inviting him home to Carrickmines for dinner afterwards and this time asked him to bring his own racquet to Fitzwilliam. I was out for revenge and practised as I had never done before or since for the game. This time I won by the narrowest of margins, to Derek's amazement. I can still recall with glee the quizzical look on his face all evening long as he repeatedly asked me, 'How did you win? You know I beat you so easily the last time'. So Derek, now you know!

The world's greatest mile was undoubtedly run in Santry Stadium on the night of 6 August 1958. It eclipsed even the White City mile. The first five men broke four minutes, with the first four breaking John Landy's official world record of 3 minutes 58 seconds. Elliott smashed the existing record by an incredible 3.5 seconds.

The result read (1) Herb Elliott (Australia) 3 min. 54.5 sec; (2) Merv Lincoln (Australia) 3 min. 55.9 sec; (3) Ron Delany (Ireland) 3 min 57.5 sec; (4) Murray Halberg (New Zealand) 3 min. 57.5 sec and (5) Albert Thomas (Australia) 3 min. 58.6 sec. Elliott and Halberg were destined to win gold in the Rome Olympics and the diminutive Thomas was to hold world two and three mile records (set in Dublin at Santry). The luckless Lincoln was probably best miler never to win a major; he lives on in sporting legend as the man who came closest to beating the invincible Elliott, who retired undefeated in the mile some years later.

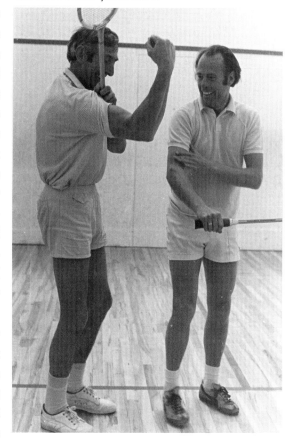

This was a magical era in Irish athletics with the world mile, and two, three and four mile records being run and set in Dublin. It was also a very special time for sports journalism in Ireland. There were great events to write about. There was an innocence, dare I say a beauty, about amateur sport and its combatants. Achievement was untarnished by issues relating to drugs, shamateurism, commercialisation, sponsorship or bitter rivalry. The sports writers rose to the task and wrote eloquently about the excitement without rancour or cynicism.

But what about the Santry Mile. I had thought beforehand that Herb Elliott was vulnerable. He had just completed an incredible mile and half-mile double at the Commonwealth Games in Cardiff. I felt he might relax a little in Dublin. I learned in Sydney many years later from my friend Albie Thomas that every detail of the race had been pre-planned and that I had been up against a Team Australia on the night. I had trained to be

Opposite left: Derek Ibbotson and I compare biceps before a game of squash at the Fitzwilliam Club.

Below: A headline after the record-breaking 880 yards in September 1960.

DELANY CHASES SNELL HOME IN RECORD-BREAKING 880

SANTRY Stadium last night resounded to the applause of an attendance of approximately 15,000 when, on the first night of Clonliffe Harriers' international sports meeting under floodlights we had record-breaking performances in the high jump, pole vault, javelin and 880 yards.

The most heart-warming performance from an Irish point of view was, however, the welcome return to something like his best form of Ronnie Delany, Ireland's Olympic representative, in the 800 metres, and the crowd rose to him to a man even though he finished only second to New Zealand's Peter Snell in the 880 yards.

Delany, a sad failure at the Olympics, was obviously out to redeem himself in front of an Irish audience, and from an early stage he was running determinedly and full of confidence.

In a fast race he lay back in the early stages as Peter Keeling led the young Crusaders' runner, Derek McCleane, with Snell close on their heels.

Delany was lying a handy fourth all through the first lap, with Herb

By S. Devlin

Elliott at his shoulder, but when Snell moved up on Keeling so, too, did Delany, and they lay thus for about 50 yards of the second lap, when the New Zealander made the first break.

Again, Delany moved with him, but the strong-running Snell opened up a five yards' gap with his sudden burst, and it took some of the Delany "kick" to bring him within striking distance. At the final bend, in fact, it looked as if Delany might possibly cause a surprise, but Snell held on to win by two yards in 1 min. 47.9 secs.

That represented a new all-comers record since it beat by .6

seconds the 1-48.5 set up by Delany in 1958. Delany himself, however, also managed to get inside his own record with a run of 1 minute 48.2, while Dr. Tony Blue, the Australian who pipped Herb Elliott for third place, was clocked at 1 minute 48.4 seconds.

Elliott's running was a complete disappointment to those who were expecting big things from the Olympic 1,500 metres champion but the fact of the matter is that the Australian has not been feeling well for the past few days and was advised yesterday by a doctor that he was possibly doing too much running.

The first record to go, however, was in the high jump when the fabulous American John Thomas cleared 7ft. 2ins. and narrowly failed in his effort to establish a new world record at 7ft. 4ins. With the start being made at 6ft. 6ins. only two competitors took part; but it was obvious that only one mattered.

Thomas cleared 6ft. 10ins. easily

able to run a sub-3 minutes 58 second mile thinking this might be enough to win. The pace was frenetic from the start and it took my best effort to merely hang-on. I was never to prove a threat.

I was sick as a parrot and disappointed after the race. And then Liam Browne the announcer said a new world record had been set. My spirits lifted when I heard my time. The disappointment of the crowd vanished when they realised they had been privileged to witness the most extraordinary mile race in the history of athletics. It was not my pleasure to be a participant for my body ached for days afterwards from the effort I had put in. I am privileged

however to have raced against the greatest miler in the world.

Years later Herb and I took part in the *Sunday Times* 'Fun Run' for various charities in Hyde Park, London. That night over dinner at our hotel with our wives Joan and Ann, he told me how Billy Morton had inveigled him to come over to Dublin for the Santry Mile immediately after the Commonwealth Games in 1958. He described meeting Billy in Cardiff and how Billy told him he had the fastest track in the world at Santry. Billy went on to claim the air quality there was also better than anywhere else, explaining that it was because of the density of trees at Santry Court. He explained that the

trees sucked up the oxygen during daylight and released it slowly during the evening, especially about the time the mile race was scheduled to start. Herb and I could only laugh at the persuasiveness of the man. The same Billy Morton persuaded Jack Crump and successive British teams to come to race in Dublin after the Second World War on the promise of copious quantities of the best Irish bacon, sausages and eggs to take back home. Later Billy was to help Brian Hewson to select a greyhound at the Shelbourne Park sales as an enticement to race against me in Dublin. The dog, I believe, went on to finish second in an English Derby in White City.

Brian Hewson was a stylist, a classical runner to watch with speed in abundance. He was equally good at the mile and half-mile. We raced six times including two major championships, the Olympic games in 1956 and the European Championships in 1958. We became and are very good friends.

We met casually twice that I can recall in the environs of major competitions. The first time was in the Olympic Village in Melbourne shortly after I had arrived in Australia. Brian was in the company of his teammates in the 1500 metres Ian Boyd and Ken Wood and enquired who I thought would win the race. They were aghast when I blandly began to explain why I thought I would win. This was not quite what they wanted or needed to hear.

Two years later on a dank and miserable day in Stockholm at the European Championships while warming up adjacent to the main stadium prior to the 1,500-metres final our paths crossed again. This time I asked the questions. 'Who do you think the conditions suit today? Brian, who do you think will win?' To my horror he said he would. The wet conditions suited him best because of his 'speed and lightness of foot'. All I can say in retrospect is 'Well done Brian, good on you!' There must be something in trying to psych one another out for he won the final going away and I finished with a wry smile on my face in third place behind Dan Waern of Sweden.

Hewson's winning time was 3 minutes 41.9 seconds, Waern ran 3 minutes 42.1 seconds and I finished in 3 minutes 42.3 seconds. Rozsavolgyi, the Hungarian world-record holder was fourth. My tactical running during the final was appalling. I dropped too far back off the pace and at one stage was thirty metres behind the race leaders. I had to work far too hard catching up down the backstretch and around the final bend to be in second place with only Waern to pass. But I had made another miscalculation. I did not

Opposite left: At the start of the Terry Fox Run for Cancer Research with Michael Wadsworth, the Canadian Ambassador to Ireland.

Above: My official accreditation for the 1958 European Championships in Stockholm.

realise that the finishing line or tape was at the end of the straight. Brian suddenly went sweeping past us both and there was no way I was going to catch him. I was disheartened afterwards that I had not won.

It was most unusual for me to be so tactically careless. It was not as if I did not rate the European Championships highly. Next to the Olympics it was the most sought after title at that time. I was competitive on the day and wanted to win, unlike in some relatively unimportant races throughout my earlier career. I can only put it down to mental tiredness at the end of a long year. From mid-January onwards I had run thirty-six races indoors and outdoors. I was at peak physical fitness, but not mentally sharp enough to win on the day.

The Irish journalists were bitterly disappointed. The fact that I had just won Ireland's first medal, be it only bronze, in a European Championship was not the story they expected to have to write about. Breaking the world record for the indoor mile in March and extending my winning streak indoors to twenty-nine straight victories seemed to be of little consequence. That magical night in Santry two weeks earlier when the world mile record was smashed by Herb Elliott did not come into the equation.

I felt hard done by the Irish sporting press. It was as if I had spoiled their party. I am not sure that they were fairly representing the viewpoint of the Irish sports fan or general public, not that it matters now. The cognoscenti were certainly more understanding of the workload I had to undertake as a scholarship athlete under the American system and during my 'summer holidays' at home in Dublin. It was after all an untarnished and amateur era in sport when elite athletes ran for the honour of winning. There were no pecuniary rewards and the commercialisation of sport, appearance money and sponsorship deals were undreamt of. I cannot recall one journalist adverting to the American 'burn out' syndrome that they had written about so passionately in my early days at Villanova.

MY ACHILLES HEEL

I was not to know it then, but 1958 marked the beginning of the end of my athletic career. I returned to Villanova in the autumn after graduating in June with a BSc. in Economics degree and being elected a member of the prestigious National Collegiate 'Who's Who?' fraternity. I chose to continue my studies towards a Master of Arts degree (on a full academic post-graduate scholarship – tuition, room and board). I no longer had any obligation to run for the university track team but could continue to train with Jumbo Elliott and his elite squad. I immersed myself in my studies but trained regularly in preparation for the indoor season.

The 1959 indoor season was brilliant. I remained undefeated and extended my winning streak to forty consecutive races. In the process I saw off the European challenge of Hewson, Waern, Rozsavolgyi and Tabori from Hungary and Zbaigniev Oxywal from Poland along with the American challengers. I broke my own world record for the mile twice in Madison Square Garden to the delight (finally!) of the New York fans. The indoor season ended in Chicago on 28 March. I decided not to race outdoors in America and to concentrate on my studies until I

Above: Commencement Day, Villanova University, 2 June 1958.

returned home to Dublin in June.

I continued to train lightly during the spring, running barefoot on the lush grass of the Villanova campus. I was intent on keeping a high level of fitness without the intensity of training on the track in preparation for a series of races in Dublin and Europe during the coming summer months. Running barefoot is as close as an athlete can get to an aesthetic experience. Your mind is free and you are in total control of your physical movement without the pressure of anyone running up your back or your coach shouting 'relax, relax; keep your arms up' or 'stop bobbing your head'. It was a joyful expression of physical self-being. It reminded me of the pleasure I had enjoyed running barefoot in College Park by kind permission of the Provost of Trinity College when I was home for the summer. Courting couples were a distraction, of course, on all campuses.

You could only avert your eyes when the petting got too torrid. Such is the dedication of the committed athlete!

Prior to returning home in early June I was staying for a few days with a friend in Atlantic City, New Jersey. For some reason I decided I had better do an interval workout at the local high school track. I donned the spikes for the first time in months and was over-zealous when running a series of repeat 220s on the sun-baked track. I seriously injured my right tendon and on my return to Dublin was unable to race or even run for months. I could barely walk and had to wear heel cushions in my shoe to alleviate the constant pain. This was despite the best of medical care from the distinguished IOC member Dr Kevin O' Flanagan, himself a rugby, soccer and athletics international.

I am reminded of the story my friend Maurice Davitt told me about his father, the

Left: The 'Delany kick' – beating Istvan Roszavolgyi (Hungary) and setting a new world indoor mile record of 4:01.4 at Madison Square Garden. My thirty-first consecutive indoor mile triumph.

Right: Training with Don Bowden on a deserted Pacific Coast beach, March 1960.

distinguished Judge Cahir Davitt and son of Thomas Davitt. Judge Davitt was a trustee of the Fitzwilliam Club, and an accomplished tennis player in his own right. He apparently seriously pulled a muscle when playing and went to his doctor for treatment. After an intensive physio session and the latest heat treatment available, his Honour enquired how long a series of such treatments would take before the injury would clear up. The doctor replied, at least one month. The supplementary question to the doctor was how long would it take if he did not take the treatment. The doctor replied at least one month. Judge Davitt determined not to waste any more of the doctor's valuable time.

Similarly, my tendonitis was going to take its own time before I could resume light training. I returned to New York in August to work for Aer Lingus as a sales representative. My responsibilities included making sales calls on Grimes Travel on Columbus Circle, the leading Irish

Below: Up the sand dunes, Pacific Coast, California.
Right: Don and I in Golden Gate Park, San Francisco.

travel agent for the fledgling airline in America. The proprietor was Paddy Grimes, who had been an outstanding inter-county footballer with Offaly in his youth. Mr Grimes insisted that I should try a raw egg with sherry every time I visited the agency. Apparently the Offaly team trained with great results on raw eggs and sherry. I was too polite to refuse and usually had to drop into the nearby New York Athletic Club, where I was a member, to sleep off the effects on a training table! Soon after, however, I took the opportunity to transfer to San Francisco, where I worked in the Aer Lingus office on Market Street, so I had to do without my sherry and egg from then on.

By now I had resumed light training in Golden Gate Park. I joined forces with Don Bowden, America's first four-minute miler, when I regained fitness and we trained together running up sand dunes in nearby San José. Don was enlisted along with Al Oerter, triple Olympic discus champion, and they had the use of a US Army jeep, which was very handy. The months seemed to rush by and my tendonitis was progressively improving.

In June I was transferred back to Aer Lingus in Dublin where I worked out of the O'Connell Street and Grafton Street offices. I continued hopefully with my preparations for the Rome Olympics, but had to take extreme care to avoid a recurrence of the injury. It was a race against time and I was to lose out by a couple of weeks. I could not afford to take the risk, on medical advice, of running a race or a time trial prior to the Games.

The Irish Olympic Council generously and in good faith selected me for the 800 metres and

Above: At my desk, Aer Lingus Office, Fifth Avenue NY (1960).
Below: In contrast, on my way to work on a foggy day in Dublin some years later.
Opposite top: My official accreditation, Rome Olympics 1960.

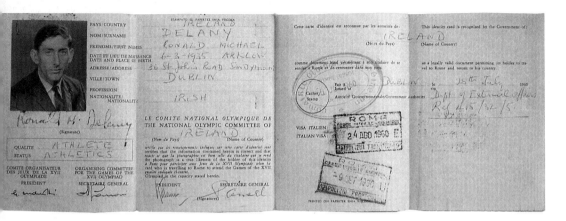

1,500 metres. My first race in Rome was on the morning of 31 August in the 800 metres, round one. I qualified comfortably in third place in a time of 1 minute 51 seconds. There was such a large entry in the event that the organisers unexpectedly decided to run the second round the same afternoon. This is not what I would have wished or indeed needed, my preparations had been so precarious all along. I ran again that evening and failed to qualify finishing in sixth place in 1 minute 51.1 seconds. It was no comfort at the time that these two races had been my first competitive outings in over a year and a half since indoors in Chicago on 28 March 1959.

I was shattered. Instinctively I asked Louis Vandendries, the athletics team manager, to scratch me from the entries for the 1,500 metres. My entry was withdrawn without argument. I had no coach, manager, mentor or advisor to persuade me otherwise. I knew in my heart that I was not fit enough to defend my 1,500-metre Olympic crown. It never occurred to me to consider running for a minor placing. Ironically, three weeks later at Santry in Dublin I ran my only other race that year. I was a close second to Peter Snell of New Zealand, the newly crowned Olympic 800-metre champion.

I finished strides ahead of Herb Elliott the winner of the 1500 metres gold medal in Rome two weeks earlier and his Australian compatriot Tony Blue. I take some consolation and pride in reviewing the photo of the finish of that race. Three Olympic Champions in the same frame. Despite the travails of the previous eighteen months and persistent injury I had demonstrated to the Irish public, and to myself, how competitive I still could be on my day.

I stayed on in Rome for the remainder of the Games and watched in awe the track and field programmes. The highlight of the Games from an Irish perspective was John Lawlor's fourth place finish in the hammer throw, keeping up the tradition of the legendary Champion Kiely, Matt McGrath, Paddy Ryan and Dr Pat O'Callaghan. It was during the Games that I first met Bob Tisdall, Ireland's gold medallist from the 1932 Los Angeles Games where he won the 400-metre hurdles.

Bob hired a bus and took the entire Irish team, boxers, fencers, runners the lot to the beach at Ostin for a day out. We sported and played all day long on the golden sands like the Bould Thady Quill. Most of us could barely swim and the fencer Harry Thuillier ventured out too far and almost drowned, which would

have been a terrible loss for Irish radio. Harry subsequently was a leading presenter of the emerging sponsored programmes on Radio Éireann. Maeve Kyle, four times Olympian for Ireland and hockey international, recounts how Bob invited her husband Sean and herself to dinner in Rome with some of his friends. The highlight of the evening was when Bob challenged one of his guests to a chariot race on the cobbled streets of Rome. They hired two carioles

– small, open, two-wheeled, horse-drawn carts – outside the restaurant. Maeve's lasting memory of the outing is of Bob standing upright in his makeshift chariot whipping his pony to victory. The same Bob Tisdall was to celebrate his eightieth birthday bungee jumping for the first time.

Bob Tisdall and Harry Thuillier became my lifelong friends. I was to meet Bob infrequently all over the world later and more especially in his adopted country, Australia, where he was

Left: Don Bowden and I take a breather while training on a beach near San José, California.

much honoured as an Olympic Champion, right up to the Sydney Games in 2000. He proudly carried the Olympic flame in the build up to the Games even though he was ninety years young at the time. We corresponded a lot and he never ceased to amuse and amaze me. A poet and an author (he wrote two unpublished books) Bob was the consummate sportsman, the true Olympian.

Bob prided himself on being able to complete a round of the local golf course in Nambour, Queensland each year not in par, but in the same score as his age. I believe only fifteen percent of all golfers can break 100 shots regularly. Bob was scoring under the 90s well into his eighties. One time he was sick and wrote to me saying 'Isn't life a bitch – I can't even play golf anymore.' He passed away, reluctantly I am sure, a few years ago in his mid-nineties leaving behind his lovely wife Peggy, his talented and caring family and a host of Olympic friends. I paraphrase one of his last messages to me – 'Now it's time for me to go, I have only one regret, I can not take my mobile phone, to call you and say not to fret.'

The last time I met Harry Thuillier was at the inaugural luncheon of the Irish Olympians Association in the RDS, Ballsbridge in 2004. It was a gala occasion, which I hosted as President of the Irish Olympians. In the company of Pat Hickey, President of the Irish Olympic Council and distinguished member of the International Olympic Committee we welcomed over two hundred Irish Olympians from all sports who had represented Ireland in successive Olympics since 1948. Our guests of honour on the day were An Taoiseach Bertie Ahern TD and the Governor of Victoria, Australia John Landy.

I regaled Harry and his beautiful wife Frances by reminding him of the time he bribed me to appear on his lunchtime radio programme by promising me a tin of the sponsor's goodies. Needless to remark Harry forgot. To his embarrassment a year later when I returned from America, I accosted him in public and rather loudly said 'Hey, Harry, where's my tin of sweets!'

The Rome Olympics were difficult for me, both physically and mentally, but at least I had the company of wonderful friends like Bob Tisdall and Harry Thuillier.

FELLOWSHIP THROUGH SPORT

I was unable to compete on the indoor circuit in America in 1961. Tendonitis kept recurring in the Achilles tendon of my right leg. It was painful in the extreme. I was not prepared to undergo continuous injections to kill that pain. Rest, or not training in my case, was the only cure and option I would take.

It was not until early July 1961 that I was fit and able to start competing again. I concentrated on the half-mile. My better performances were racing against George Kerr of Jamaica and Peter Snell, the Olympic champion. I ran a new national record for the 800 metres of 1 minute 47.1 seconds in Santry Stadium when finishing a close third to Snell and Kerr. This augured well for the upcoming Universiade or World University Championships to be held in Sofia, Bulgaria. I eventually

managed to beat George Kerr in a slow half-mile race on a blustery July day in Cardiff. Peter Snell of New Zealand was to remain the only middle distance Olympic champion or elite contemporary athlete that I was unable to avenge defeat against in my entire running career. I don't lose sleep at night over it for in my opinion he was the greatest ever half-miler/miler in the history of middle-distance running.

Prior to travelling to represent Ireland at the Universiade in Sofia. I had the pleasure of being part of an Irish 4 x 880 yards, or two-mile, relay team that set a new European record for the distance of 7 minutes 21.8 seconds in Santry. Basil Clifford (Donore Harriers) ran leadoff; Derek McCleane (Crusaders AC) the second

Above: Ireland's 4x880 yards relay team that broke the European record at Santry, 8 August 1961 with a time of 7:21.8, (l-r) Derek McCleane (Crusaders AC), Noel Carroll (Civil Service) and Basil Clifford (Donore Harriers).

leg; Noel Carroll the rising young star from Civil Service AC the third; and I brought home the baton. The following night I was to run the last mile race of my career comfortably beating Ken Wood of Britain in a slowing 4 minutes 04.3 seconds. Significantly and ominously for my rivals in Sofia I ran the last lap in a blistering 55.3 seconds. I had peaked and regained absolute fitness once again in spite of my recurring injuries and interestingly while based in Dublin.

The World University Championships, or Universiade as it was called then, was confined to contemporary university graduates. It was comparable to a European Championships because it was open to athletes from all around the world. I won the 800-metres gold medal in a slow tactical final. The next day I opted out of running in the 1,500 metres and completing the double, although I was favourite to win. The reason why is simple. I went out to dinner at a beautiful restaurant called The Swans to celebrate my win and was partying with my fellow athletes. Come the time to leave to get a good nights sleep in preparation for the 1500-metre heats I had to make a decision. Should I stay at the party or run in the 1500 metres? The party won.

I tell this story because it best illustrates the sporting times and fellowship I was so lucky to enjoy throughout my career. I was an amateur athlete and there was no question of being paid to run. Material reward or money was not a consideration. Athletics was yet to become commercialised and later on a professional sport. The question of product endorsements, fee payments or appearance money did not arise. There was no opportunity for 'Ronnie Delany' to become an international brand in the marketing jargon of today. Besides I now had won medals in every major championship I had competed in. I had no team manager or coach with me in Sofia to influence my decision one way or other.

This does pose the question of whether I would have liked to have been a professional athlete competing in today's competitive environment with its attendant opportunity to maximise your potential earnings and become a multi-millionaire. I have absolutely no problem with today's athletes in any sport being paid to perform. It is not a case of 'either/or'. If I was competing now I am sure money would be a further incentive and motivational factor to strive to be the best athlete in the world. Olympic ideals and material reward are not mutually exclusive. Just look at how the world's greatest professional athletes want to take part in the Olympics for the honour of representing their countries and winning the most exclusive and elusive title in the world – Olympic Champion.

Paul Kimmage, the distinguished sports journalist and exemplary sportsman, asked me, at the end of a long interview for the *Sunday Tribune*, 'What would it be like if you were running now, Ronnie?' I recall we were standing outside Fitzwilliam where we had just finished lunch. I think I replied along the following lines, 'Paul, I would probably offer you a lift back to your office in Baggot Street in my Rolls Royce!' In the course of the subsequent profile piece in the *Tribune*, Paul also mentioned my preference for Tipperary Water over the other brands. The next day caseloads of Tipperary Water were delivered to my office at Fitzwilliam Square. A sign of the different times perhaps – nothing like that ever happened in my running days!

The Irish two-mile relay team were invited to take part in the indoor season in America in a series of relay races, on the strength of setting the European record. We trained hard together prior to going over to New York in late January. We became a close-knit team and friends. Based at the Paramount Hotel off Broadway we had a great time attending the shows and meeting the stars. Billy Morton was our team manager. He arranged a side trip for us to the White House and an appointment to meet President J. F.

Kennedy, which the President was unable to fulfil on the day. However we enjoyed a wonderful tour of the White House and the Oval Office. We had the opportunity to sit on the President's rocking chair, which now adorns Shanahan's Restaurant on St Stephen's Green.

The irrepressible Morton was a dream discovery

Below: Members of the Irish relay team drop in to see me at the Aer Lingus stand at a trade show in New York, 1962 (l-r) Billy Morton, Derek McCleane, Basil Clifford and Tom O'Riordan.

We won successive races in New York, The Boston Garden, Philadelphia's Convention Hall and New York again. Noel Carroll had commenced his studies as a scholarship athlete at Villanova University so he joined the team each week-end for the races. The next race we had was in the New York Knights of Columbus meet in Madison Square

Left: The Irish relay team arrive in New York for the indoor season, 1962 (l-r) Derek McCleane, Ron Delany, Basil Clifford (front) and Noel Carroll.
Below: Meeting Elaine Stritch backstage at Noel Coward's Broadway hit Sail Away, *(l-r) Basil, me, Tom and Derek.*
Opposite right: A relaxed moment at home in South Park, Foxrock with Lisa and Ronnie.

for the US media and gave some hilarious interviews. My funniest moment was when I had to explain to him that we should fly up to Boston and not take a taxi as he was suggesting. It was a very special time being with Billy, Basil Clifford – who was killed tragically in a munitions explosion in a Birmingham factory – and the late Noel Carroll, who loved to run more than any other man I ever knew. Derek McCleane and I, in mourning their passing, celebrate their memory as great athletes with whom we were proud to share the honour of representing our country and the joy of relay racing and victory.

Garden. We faced a Canadian team anchored by an outstanding runner, Bill Crothers. The boys did their job as usual and handed me the stick or baton in the lead. Crothers ran me down on the last lap and we suffered our only defeat.

I was privileged to have had the opportunity towards the end of my career to run on such an outstanding Irish relay team and to enjoy the friendship and good humour of my team mates at the time.

I had a recurrence of the Achilles problem after the race and was unable to race again that winter. The team stayed on in America and Derek McCleane went on to win a great 1,000-yards race in Vancouver, BC in a record time, Noel Carroll began an illustrious athletics and

business career and Basil Clifford was to subsequently become the second Irishman in history to run a four-minute mile.

I was never to race again and during the summer of 1962 I announced my retirement from athletics and my engagement to Joan Riordan on the same day. I was to be bountifully blessed once again, for Joan and I have enjoyed a loving and fulfilled relationship to this day. Our four children Lisa, Ronnie, Jennifer and Michelle, and their partners, have brought us nothing but happiness. It is so simplistic to say these things, but any grandparent will understand our joy in having fifteen beautiful grandchildren. The loss at birth of Lisa and John's second child, little Johnny, brought home to us the preciousness of

in my office at the beginning of the millennium year. He told me the *Independent* readers had voted me overwhelmingly as the Champion of Champions of the past half-century. I was delighted with James Hanley's larger-than-life portrait of me, which was hung in the same year as part of the Portrait Collection of the National Gallery of Ireland on Merrion Street. It is a realistic work that somehow captures me as I am today, but suggests my sporting past. The first time I saw the portrait privately in James' studio I felt I was looking into my soul. It was an eerie feeling, but one with good vibes; I was comfortable with what I saw. I was more amused at the official unveiling when the then chairperson of the National Gallery, Carmel Naughton remarked, 'the only other athlete to

life. Johnny's gift to us was to bring us closer together as a family and to remind us constantly of the frailty of life and of God's will.

Looking back on my life and my athletic career I can have no regrets. I won and lost races, but one day I climbed to the top of Mount Olympus. That seems to be the thing that has mattered most; as that real Dub once wittily said when he recognised me years later walking along Dublin's North Wall, 'I never saw anyone get so much mileage out of winning a bloody medal!'

He was right of course. I have received every conceivable honour from my peers and from the Irish public at large. I appreciate every Irish or international honour in its own way, for each one means something different to me and to my legacy to sport. I was humbled and proud when John Comyn of the *Irish Independent* phoned me

be hung in the Gallery was Master McGrath – the legendary greyhound who won the Waterloo Cup.'

As a child I was a keen philatelist, so I was very pleased when the Dominican Republic selected me for inclusion in an Olympic series featuring gold medallists from the 1956 Olympic Games in Melbourne. Then in 1984, the year of the Los Angeles Olympics, I was honoured by the Irish Government when An Post issued a series of stamps commemorating Ireland's gold medal achievements. The stamps commemorated Dr Pat O'Callaghan's successes in the 1928 and 1932 Olympics and Bob Tisdall's win in 1932, along with my victory in 1956. The graphic illustrations depicted us competing in our prime. At the launch of the stamps in the Gresham Hotel, while the formal speeches were going on, Dr Pat turned to me and asked in his inimitable way 'Who drew the pictures?' I replied 'Louis Le Brocquy, the distinguished artist.' To which Pat retorted, 'He knows damn-all about hammer throwing!' Conversely, I was delighted with Louis' depiction of me. His illustration made me look like a classical runner straight off a Grecian urn.

This year I was delighted to formally receive the Freedom of the City of Dublin from our most honourable Lord Mayor Councillor Catherine Byrne and her fellow Councillors. It was a very special day of joyous celebration for me, my loving family and relations, my friends who have been supportive all my life and my fellow Olympians.

What a privilege it is for me and my fellow honouree Sir Bob Geldof to follow in the footsteps of such an illustrious list of previous recipients. I willingly accepted the honour with humility and a deep sense of indebtedness to the Lord Mayor and the City Council. I am greatly honoured to be enjoined in Dublin's history with former Presidents, national and international statesmen, literary, arts, musical and cultural figures along with the iconic sportsmen of more recent years.

I promised not to abuse the privileges

Opposite top: The Melvin A. Traylor trophy for the Bankers Mile, won 28 March 1958.
Opposite bottom: James Hanley RHA's portrait of me for the National Gallery Millennium Series, sponsored by Irish Life.
Below: The 1984 Olympic stamps first day cover autographed by the three Irish Olympic Champions.

bestowed upon me, but I am tempted to check out the availability of commonage. I have had no end of offers of free sheep from my country relations and farmers all over Ireland. I will of course defend the city from attack, but I am having some difficulty acquiring a longbow made of yew and twelve arrows of the same wood.

I am a Dubliner. My athletic career and life are intrinsically linked to my native city. The people of Dublin have always warmly applauded my achievements and treated me as one of their own. This, over the years, was sometimes to the bemusement of American friends or new business associates visiting Dublin for the first time. They had to come to terms with everyone on the street who recognised me saying 'Hello', and with newspaper and flower sellers or Gardaí on the beat enquiring

Top: Freedom of the City, 5 March 2006, with Sir Bob Geldof.

Bottom: The extended Delany family with the Lord Mayor of Dublin, Cllr Catherine Byrne at the Freedom of the City ceremony, 2006.

after my health by asking 'How ya, Ronnie!'

It would take far too long to enumerate the sporting awards I have received over the past fifty years. However the role these awards play in perpetuating the mythical history and ideals of sport cannot be underestimated. They create special social occasions for the various sporting organisations and athletes to interact in fellowship along with the guest of the sponsors. Goodwill abounds and the stars of one sport can meet and get to know the super-stars of another code. Believe me there is a mutuality between champion athletes and a compatibility that requires no explanation. We are usually strangely mute about our own sporting careers but want to know more about the accomplishments of the others we so admire.

I would single out the annual Texaco Sports Stars Awards established in 1958 as such a unique and gala occasion celebrating Irish sporting achievements since then. However, even Olympians attending gala events are not immune to traffic laws; after the most recent Texaco Awards, I came out to find my car clamped! It was my own fault entirely, but the problem was I was carrying no credit cards, which are an essential requirement if you

wanted to expedite a quick release. Luckily for me, Keith Wood, the lionhearted rugby champion, came to my rescue, used his credit card to secure my release and I was on my way home in less than an hour. I sent him a cheque and a thank you note the next day. If only I got park-

Below: Welcoming the most legendary Olympian Jesse Owens (USA) to Dublin. Snubbed by Hitler, Jesse went on to win four gold medals at the Berlin Olympics in 1936.

Top: A galaxy of 1,500-metre stars meet in Sydney, 1999, (l-r, gold medallists' year of victory in brackets), Herb Elliott (1960), John Landy, John Walker (1976), Steve Cram, Ronnie Delany (1956), Kip Keino (1968), Peter Snell (1964).
Above: Accepting a presentation from Syd Grange, President of the AOC, at the twenty-fifth anniversary dinner in Melbourne. Betty Cuthbert (winner of four gold medals) looks on.

ing concessions with the Freedom of the City; free grazing for my sheep on Dublin's commonage is of little value to me!

An Olympian is an Olympian forever, and apart from successive Olympic Games there are frequent opportunities for us to get together around the world. I was honoured to be invited as a guest to the Sydney and Athens Games by Pat Hickey, President of the Irish Olympic Council, and his Executive Committee. I meet countless Olympians attending World Olympians Associations (WOA) events and conferences in my capacity as President of the Irish Olympians Association (IOA). The WOA is the fourth tier in the structure of the Olympic Movement and is an association of almost 100,000 Olympians. The recently formed IOA has over five hundred members who have represented Ireland in successive Olympic Games since London in 1948. Villanova lists over a hundred alumni who have represented their countries at the Olympics. We had a marvellous reunion and assembly at Villanova in October 2004 organised by Marcus O'Sullivan, the Head Track Coach and former World Champion.

I am often asked do I keep in contact with the finalists in the 1500 metres in Melbourne 1956. Fortunately I am in a position to say, 'We have and we do to this very day.' John Landy, former distinguished Governor of the State of Victoria, and I have developed our special friendship since I had my first opportunity to revisit Melbourne in 1981 as a guest of the Australian Olympic Committee on the twenty-fifth anniversary of the Melbourne Games. The AOC had another celebration party on the thirtieth anniversary that we were also at. We subsequently worked closely together supporting the Melbourne bid to host the 1992 Games and the successful Sydney 2000 bid. I have met up with Merv Lincoln on many occasions. Brian Hewson, my English foe, and I meet occasionally in Ireland and Spain. Murray Halberg is founder of the Halberg Trust in New Zealand and as fellow Olympic gold medallists we meet intermittently. I see Lazslo Tabori of Hungary in America, where he now lives.

It is more difficult to maintain contact with my non-English speaking 1,500-metres rivals. The best that Klaus Richtzenhain of Germany who finished second, and I can do is exchange

Above: Judy Patching, official starter 1956 Olympics, points out the starting line for the 1,500 metres in the Olympic Stadium some twenty-five years later.

Speaking at the 1982 Texaco Sports Star Awards Banquet in Dublin after accepting the Hall of Fame award.

Christmas cards. I think it is a feature of the golden decade in miling (1954-1964) that the protagonists became lasting friends. During that era we competed hard on the track against each other, won and lost, but there was no animosity afterwards. I can proudly claim friendship then and since with my archrivals and contemporaries in sport whether they were American, Australian, British or European.

There was one unique occasion for a get-together, masterminded by Ron Clarke who at eighteen years of age carried the Olympic torch on its final leg into the MCC Grounds, climbed the stadium steps and lit the Olympic flame to open the XVIth Olympiad in Melbourne. Ron became even more renowned when he subsequently set twenty-seven world records in various distances on the track. In the mid-nineties he became involved with Chuck Feeney the American philanthropist in the development of an ecological resort near Queensland on the Gold Coast at an estimated cost of 200 million Australian dollars.

The resort was due to open in 1998. People thought Ron was mad at the time for he decided to mark the occasion by inviting all the Melbourne

1,500-metre finalists to Couran Cove Resort, Stradbroke Island for the official opening on 15 September. Seven of the twelve-man field accepted – me, Landy, Hewson, Tabori, Lincoln, Halberg and Scott. It was such fun for us all and what a time we had together.

The media, I think it is fair to say, went wild at the opportunity to meet these almost antediluvian athletes who may have lost the spring in our step but not the sparkle in our eyes. Our memories were intact and we were to entertain readers, listeners and viewers with our anecdotal memories of times past when sport was somehow different. Ron Clarke was not considered so mad after all for the media coverage was sentimental perhaps, but expansive in its praise for Couran Cove Resort, its rainforests, nature resort, trekking trails, marinas, surf club and state of the art sports facilities.

I am invited back to Australia in November 2006 for another reunion on the fiftieth anniversary of the opening of the 1956 Games. Joan and I will be the guests of Pat Hickey and the Executive Committee of the Olympic Council of Ireland and my Australian friends on the Victorian Olympic Reunion Committee. It is going to be some party!

The 1956 Olympic finalists enjoy a reunion in Couran Cove, Queensland, forty-two years later, (l-r) Merv Lincoln (Australia), Murray Halberg (New Zealand), Neville Scott (New Zealand), Brian Hewson (Britain), Lazslo Tabori (Hungary), John Landy (Australia) and Ron Delany (Ireland), with our host, Ron Clarke.

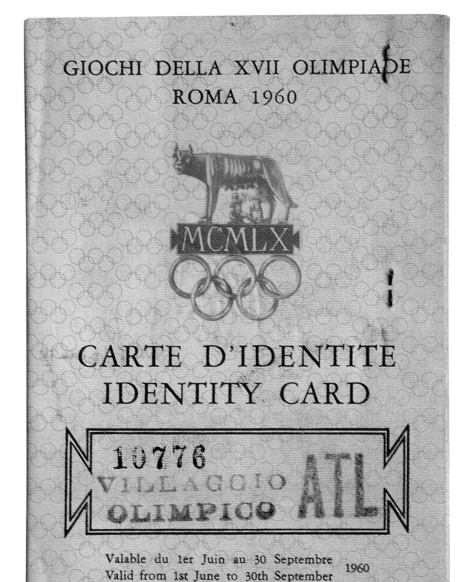

GIOCHI DELLA XVII OLIMPIADE
ROMA 1960

MCMLX

CARTE D'IDENTITE
IDENTITY CARD

10776
VILLAGGIO ATL
OLIMPICO

Valable du 1er Juin au 30 Septembre
Valid from 1st June to 30th September 1960

196

CAREER SUMMARY

BY TONY O'DONOGHUE

Tony O'Donoghue is a member of Crusaders AC. He has always had a keen interest in the achievements of fellow competitors and has been collating and documenting their times and placements for many years; in 1959 he joined the influential Association of Track and Field Statisticians.

He researched and compiled the first detailed listing of the best Irish performances, publishing the Irish All-Time List in 1961. He has also extensively researched the social dimensions of the early development of athletics in the late nineteenth and early twentieth centuries in Ireland.

As a commentator on live track and field for RTÉ, he has worked on every Olympic Games since 1972, every European Championships since 1971 and many World Championships.

DATE	MEET	LOCATION	EVENT	TIME	PLACED	NOTES
1952						
13-May	Leinster Colleges, Qual.	Iveagh Grounds, Dublin	880 Yards	2m 14.4s	(1)	
17-May	Leinster Colleges, Finals	Iveagh Grounds, Dublin	880 Yards	2m 06.6s	(1)	
24-May	All-Ireland Colleges Mardyke,	Cork	880 Yards	2m 03.9s	(1)	
02-Jun	AAU Youths C'ship	Shelbourne Stadium, Dublin	880 Yards	2m 04.4s	(1)	
14-Jun	All Ireland Youths	Shelbourne Stadium, Dublin	880 Yards	2m 04.0s	(1)	

DATE	MEET	LOCATION	EVENT	TIME	PLACED	NOTES
1953						
15-May	Leinster Coll. Qual.	Iveagh Grounds, Dublin.	440 Yards	54s.	(1)	
15-May	Leinster Coll. Qual.	Iveagh Grounds, Dublin.	880 Yards	2m 08.9s	(1)	
22-May	Leinster Coll. Finals	Iveagh Grounds, Dublin.	440 Yards	...	(2)	L.Moloney, Roscrea, won 53.1s
22-May	Leinster Coll. Finals	Iveagh Grounds, Dublin.	880 Yards	2m 07.5s	(1)	
25-May	All-Ireland Colleges	Tuam	440 Yards	...	(2)	L.Moloney, Roscrea, won 53.6s
25-May	All-Ireland Colleges	Tuam	880 Yards	2m 07.4s	(1)	
06-Jun	AAU Youths C'ship.	Shelbourne Stadium	880 Yards	2m 06.5s	(1)	
14-Jul	Crusaders A.C. meet	College Park, Dublin	880 Yards	2m 04.3s	(1)	
06-Aug	Clonliffe Harriers meet	College Park, Dublin	880 Yards***	1m 55.5s***	(1)	*** Handicap event. Allowance 20y.
22-Aug	AAU v. NIAAA match	College Park, Dublin	880 Yards	1m 58.7s	(1)	First senior win.

DATE	MEET	LOCATION	EVENT	TIME	PLACED	NOTES
1954						
11-Jun	AAU Championships	Shelbourne Stadium, Dublin	880 Yards	1m 54.7s NR	(1)	Dick Mackay, Michael Byrne
15-Jun	Clonliffe Invitational	College Park, Dublin	880 Yards	1m 53.7s NR	(1)	Paul Raudenbush, Penn; D.Pratt, Cornell.
26-Jun	All-Ireland Championship	Shelbourne Stadium, Dublin	880 Yards	1m 58.0s	(1)	Dermot O'Loughlin
03-Jul	Donore Invitational	College Park, Dublin	880 Yards	1m 54.5s	(1)	Victor Milligan
17-Jul	Irl. & Sco.V Eng. & Wal.	White City, London	880 Yards	1m 54.3s	(2)	Derek Johnson
21-Jul	Donore Invitational	College Park, Dublin	4 x 440 Yards	(49.5s)	(1)	Crusaders team set new IR. 3rd leg. Cormac O'Cleirigh, Philip Godden, RMD, David Godden.
28-Jul	Graded meeting	Shelbourne Stadium, Dublin	440 Yards	51.0s	(1)	
30-Jul	**Clonliffe Invitational**	**College Park, Dublin**	**880 Yards**	**1m 53.2s NR**	**(1)**	**Lang Stanley, David Godden.**
02-Aug	AAU v AAA Wales	Maindy Stadium, Cardiff	880 Yards	2m 01.5s	(1)	J.G.Williams, Wales
04-Aug	Clonliffe Invitational	College Park, Dublin	880 Yards	1m 54.0s	(1)	Lang Stanley; Dermot O'Loughlin (1m 55.2s)
25-Aug	**European Championships**	**Berne**	**800 Metres, ht.4**	**1m 51.8s NR**	**(2)**	**Roger Moens**
27-Aug	**European Championships**	**Berne**	**800 Metres, sf1**	**1m 50.2s NR**	**(2)**	Lajos Szentgali. (de Muynck, ...Hewson)
28-Aug	European Championships	Berne	800 Metres	2m 03.5s	(8)	
18-Sep	Clonliffe Invitational	College Park, Dublin	880 Yards	1m 57.8s	(1)	William Aylett, GB

DATE 1955	MEET	LOCATION	EVENT	TIME	PLACED	NOTES
15-Jan	Boston Knights of C.	Boston, indoor	1000 Yards	2m 10.2s	(1)	
21-Jan	Philadelphia Inquirer	Philadelphia, ind.	1000 Yards	2m 16.7s	(1)	Tom Courtney
05-Feb	Millrose Games	Madison Sq. Gdns., NY	880 Yards	1m 53.0s	(2)	Audun Boysen
19-Feb	US AAU Indoor C'ships	Madison Sq. Gdns., NY	1000 Yards, ht.2	2m 14.3s	(1)	
19-Feb	US AAU Indoor C'ships	Madison Sq. Gdns., NY	1000 Yards	2m 17.2s	(4)	Arnie Sowell, Audun Boysen, Tom Courtney
05-Mar	NY Knights of Columbus	Madison Sq. Gdns., NY	1000 Yards	2m 10.1s	(1)	Tom Courtney
20-May	**LA Coliseum Relays**	**Los Angeles Coliseum**	**880 Yards**	**1m 50.4s NR**	(1)	**Lon Spurrier, Lang Stanley, Mal Whitfield. Tom Courtney (1m 50.3s) was Disq.**
15-Jun	Invitational	College Park, Dublin	880 Yards	1m 51.0s	(2)	Derek Johnson, 1m 50.8s
16-Jun	Clonliffe Invitational	College Park, Dublin	440 Yards	50.1s	(1)	R. Skerritt, Yale.
21-Jun	AAU Championships	College Park, Dublin	440 Yards	49.8s	(1)	Philip Godden
02-Jul	All Ireland Championships	Dunmore, Belfast	880 Yards	2m 02.9s	(1)	
14-Jul		(Brussels 800 Metres)	1m 50.6	1m 50.6	(2)	Roger Moens
		(880 Yards)	1m 51.2s			

DATE 1955	MEET	LOCATION	EVENT	TIME	PLACED	NOTES
21-Jul	Invitational	College Park, Dublin	880 Yards	1m 50.0s NR	(1)	Derek Johnson, 1m 50.2s
04-Aug	Clonliffe Harriers meet	College Park, Dublin	1500 Metres	3m 49.9s		
			1 Mile	4m 05.8s	(1)	
14-Oct	Villanova v Pitt. C-C.	Villanova	5 1/4 Miles	28m 12s	(2)	Alex Breckenridge, 27m 45s
05-Nov	Villanova v Quantico C-C.	Villanova		27m 15.5s	(=1)	Alex Breckenridge,
14-Nov	IC4A Cross Country	Van Cortland Park, NY		24m 53s	(2)	Henry Kennedy. MSU, 24m 30.3s

DATE 1956	MEET	LOCATION	EVENT	TIME	PLACED	NOTES	
14-Jan	Boston Knights of C.	Boston, indoor	1 Mile	4m 11.2s	(1)	Len Truex	2
20-Jan	Philadelphia Inquirer	Philadelphia, ind.	1 Mile	4m 16.9s	(1)	Len Truex	3
28-Jan	67th annual Boston AA	Boston, indoor	1 Mile	4m 06.3s	(1)	Len Truex, Joe Deady, Wes Santee	4
04-Feb	Millrose Games	Madison Sq. Gdns., NY	1 Mile	4m 09.5s	(1)	Len Truex	5
11-Feb	NYAC Games	Madison Sq. Gdns., NY	1 Mile	4m 14.0s	(1)	George King, Len Truex, Joe Deady	6
18-Feb	US AAU Indoor C'ships	Madison Sq. Gdns., NY	1 Mile	4m 14.5s	(1)	Bill Squires	7
25-Feb	IC4A Indoor	Madison Sq. Gdns., NY	1 Mile	4m 11.4s	(1)	Ike Matza	8

DATE 1956	MEET	LOCATION	EVENT	TIME	PLACED	NOTES	
03-Mar	NY Knights of Columbus	Madison Sq. Gdns., NY	I Mile	4m 11.8s	(1)	George King	9
28-Apr	Penn Relays	Philadelphia	4 x 440 Yards	(48.4s)	(1)	3rd leg	
28-Apr	Penn Relays	Philadelphia	Sprint Medley	...	(1)	4th leg	
28-Apr	Penn Relays	Philadelphia	Distance Medley	(4m 09.6s)	(1)	4th leg, I Mile.	
6-7 Apr	Marine Relays	Quantico, Va.	4 x 440 Yards	...	(2)	not clear which leg.	
6-7 Apr	Marine Relays	Quantico, Va.	4 x I Mile	(4m 25.1s)	(3)	4th leg	
6-7 Apr	Marine Relays	Quantico, Va.	Distance Medley	(4m 14.2s)	(1)	4th leg	
14-Apr		West Chester	I Mile	4m 04.9s NR	(1)	Personal Best;	
05-May		Los Angeles	I Mile	4m 05.5s	(3)	Jim Bailey, 3m 58.6s, John Landy, 3m 58.7s	
12-May	West Coast Relays	Fresno, Ca.	I Mile	4m 09.2s	(2)	John Landy, 3m 59.1s	
15-May	Villanova	Vilanova v La Salle	880 Yards	1m 54.9s	(1)		
26-May	IC4A Outdoor	Randall's Island, NY	I Mile	4m 14.4s	(1)		
27-May	IC4A Outdoor	Randall's Island, NY	880 Yards	1m 52.0s	(2)	Arnie Sowell, 1m 51.1s	
01-Jun	Compton Invitational	Compton, Ca.	I Mile	3m 59.0s NR	(1)	Gunnar Nielsen, Fred Dwyer, Bobby Seaman	
02-Jun	Pacific AAU	Stockton, Ca.	880 Yards	1m 49.5s NR	(1)	Lang Stanley, Dick Foerster, Lonnie Spurrier	
16-Jun	NCAA	Berkeley, Ca.	1500 Metres	3m 47.3s	(1)	Jim Bailey, Sid Wing, Bobby Seaman	
23-Jun	All Ireland Championships	College Park, Dublin	880 Yards	1m 53.0s	(1)		
25-Jun	Invitational	Lansdowne Road, Dublin	I Mile	4m 07.0s	(2)	Brian Hewson. 4m 07.0s. Disputed decision Intervals 61s; 2m 03s; 3m 08s.	
04-Jul	Civil Service Invitational	College Park, Dublin	I Mile	4m 07.5s	(1)	Graham Everett, UK.	
07-Jul	AAU Championships	College Park, Dublin	440 Yards	49.5s	(1)	Garry Dempsey; Philip Godden	
08-Jul	Invitational	Paris	800m	dnf		spiked after 100m. Dnf.	
06-Aug		London	I Mile	4m 06.4s	(3)	Derek Ibbotson, Ian Boyd	
10-Aug	Clonliffe Invitational	Lansdowne Road, Dublin	I Mile	4m 20s u.	(2)	Hewson, 4m 06.1s.	
29-Nov	Olympic Games MCG,	Melbourne	1500 Metres, ht.2	3m 47.7s	(3)		
01-Dec	Olympic Games MCG,	Melbourne	1500 Metres	3m 41.2s OR; NR	(1)	Klaus Richtzenhain, John Landy, Laszlo Tabori, Brian Hewson, Stan Jungwirth, Neville Scott, Ian Boyd.	

DATE 1957	MEET	LOCATION	EVENT	TIME	PLACED	NOTES	
02-Feb	Boston AA	Boston	1 Mile	4m 07.5	(1)	Bobby Seaman	10
09-Feb	Millrose Games	Madison Sq. Gdns., NY	1 Mile	4m 06.7s	(1)	Laszlo Tabori, Bobby Seaman	11
16-Feb	NYAC Games	Madison Sq. Gdns., NY	1 Mile	4m 06.8s	(1)	Fred Dwyer, Jim Beatty	12
23-Feb	US AAU Indoor C'ships	Madison Sq. Gdns., NY	1 Mile	4m 07.0s	(1)	Laszlo Tabori, Fred Dwyer	13
02-Mar	IC4A Indoor	Madison Sq. Gdns., NY	1000 Yards, ht	2m 14.0s	(1)		
02-Mar	IC4A Indoor	Madison Sq. Gdns., NY	1000 Yards	2m 14.0s	(1)	Ike Matza	14
02-Mar	IC4A Indoor	Madison Sq. Gdns., NY	2 Miles	9m 06.6s	(1)	Lew Stieglitz. Win streak indoor now 15.	15
09-Mar	NY Knights of Columbus	Madison Sq. Gdns., NY	1 Mile	4m 09.2s	(1)	Burr Grim	16
16-Mar	Chicago Daily News	Chicago	1 Mile	4m 03.8s	(1)	Burr Grim, Ted Wheeler, Laszlo Tabori	17
22-Mar	Cleveland	Knights of C. Cleveland	1 Mile	4m 10.4s	(1)	Jim Beatty, Ted Wheeler	18
13-Apr	Queen's – Iona Relays	New York	Sprint Medley	(1m 54.0s)	(1)	4th leg	
13-Apr	Queen's – Iona Relays	New York	4 x 440 Yards	...	(1)	4th leg, 'fast'.	
20-Apr	vs Navy, Penn State	Villanova	1 Mile	4m 12.4s	(1)		
20-Apr	vs Navy, Penn State	Villanova	880 Yards	1m 55.5s	(1)		
26-Apr	Penn Relays	Philadelphia	Distance Medley	...	(1)	4th leg	
27-Apr	Penn Relays	Philadelphia	4 x 440 Yards	(48.0s)	(1)	3rd leg	
27-Apr	Penn Relays	Philadelphia	Sprint Medley	...	(1)	4th leg	
04-May	vs La Salle		880 Yards	1m 53.5s	(1)		
11-May	Villanova v Seton Hall	Villanova	1 Mile	4m 06.7s	(1)		
11-May	Villanova v Seton Hall	Villanova	880 Yards	1m 55.5s	(1)		
25-May	vs Quantico		880 Yards	1m 50.3s	(1)		
25-May	vs Quantico		1 Mile	4m 14.1s	(1)		
01-Jun	IC4A Outdoor	Randall's Island, New York	880 Yards	1m 49.5s =NR	(1)	Tom Murphy	
01-Jun	IC4A Outdoor	Randall's Island, New York	1 Mile	4m 08.4s	(1)	James Doulin	
08-Jun	Meet of Champions	Houston	1 Mile	4m 05.4s	(1)	Gail Hodgson, Joe Villareal	

DATE 1957	MEET	LOCATION	EVENT	TIME	PLACED	NOTES
08-Jun	Meet of Champions	Houston	880 Yards	1m 48.4s NR	(1)	Tom Courtney; 45 minutes interval
14-Jun	NCAA Outdoor	Austin	880 Yards, ht 2	1m 52.1s	(1)	
15-Jun	NCAA Outdoor	Austin	1 Mile	4m 06.5s	(1)	Jim Grelle, Burr Grim
15-Jun	**NCAA Outdoor**	**Austin**	**880 Yards**	**1m 47.8s NR**	**(2)**	**Don Bowden, 1m 47.2s. 35 minutes interval from mile. RMD Splits - 54.9s + 52.9s.**
22-Jun	Clonliffe Invitational	Lansdowne Road, Dublin	1 Mile	4m 09.7s	(1)	Brian Hewson, Gordon Pirie
26-Jun	AAU Championships	Lansdowne Road, Dublin	880 Yards	1m 56.0s	(1)	Paul Toomey, Derek McCleane. Sodden track.
29-Jun	All-Ireland Championships	Paisley Park, Belfast	880 Yards	1m 49.9y	(1)	Charlie McAlinden. First quarter 54s.
06-Jul	Civil Service Invitational	College Park, Dublin	1 Mile	4m 04.7s	(1)	Mike Berisford, 4m 04.8s; Graham Everett, 4m 05.3s
12-Jul	AAA Championships	White City, London	880 Yards heat	1m 54.1s	(1)	
13-Jul	AAA Championships	White City, London	880 Yards	1m 49.6s	(1)	Mike Rawson, Ted Buswell
16-Jul	Donore Invitational	College Park, Dublin	880 Yards	1m 50.2s	(1)	Jim Patterson, UK
19-Jul	**Invitational**	**London**	**1 Mile**	**3m 58.8s NR**	**(2)**	**Derek Ibbotson 3m 57.2s WR; (Stan Jungwirth, Ken Wood, Stefan Lewandowski.)**
			1500 Metres	3m 42.4s		
24-Jul	Rehab Invitational	Lansdowne Road, Dublin	880 Yards	1m 55.0s	(1)	
29-Jul	Invitational	Lansdowne Road, Dublin	1 Mile	4m 05.4s	(1)	Derek Ibbotson

DATE 1958	MEET	LOCATION	EVENT	TIME	PLACED	NOTES	
18-Jan	Mass. Knights of C.	Boston	1 Mile	4m 05.0s	(1)	Phil Coleman	19
24-Jan	Philadelphia Inquirer	Philadelphia	1 Mile	4m 08.1s	(1)	Phil Coleman	20
01-Feb	Boston AA	Boston	1 Mile	4m 05.3s	(1)	Jim Beatty	21
08-Feb	Millrose Games	Madison Sq. Gdns., NY	1 Mile	4m 04.6s	(1)	George King	22
15-Feb	NYAC Games	Madison Sq. Gdns., NY	1 Mile	4m 10.0s	(1)	Istvan Rozsavolgyi, Jim Grelle, Burr Grim	23
22-Feb	US AAU Indoor C'ships	Madison Sq. Gdns., NY	1 Mile	4m 03.7s	(1)	Istvan Rozsavolgyi, Jim Grelle, George King	24
01-Mar	IC4A Indoor	Madison Sq. Gdns., NY	1000 Yards, ht.	2m 12.6s	(1)		
01-Mar	IC4A Indoor	Madison Sq. Gdns., NY	1000 Yards	2m 12.8s	(1)		25
01-Mar	IC4A Indoor	Madison Sq. Gdns., NY	2 Miles	9m 17.6s	(1)		26
08-Mar	NY Knights of Columbus	Madison Sq. Gdns., NY	1 Mile	4m 08.4s	(1)	Phil Coleman, Burr Grim, Jim Beatty	27
14-Mar	**Chicago Daily News**	**Chicago**	**1 Mile**	**4m 03.4s WR**	**(1)**	**Phil Coleman, Burr Grim, Jim Beatty**	**28**
21-Mar	Cleveland Knights of C.	Cleveland	1 Mile	4m 12.7s	(1)	Burr Grim, Arnie Sowell	29
12-Apr	Quantico Relays	Quantico, Va.	Distance Medley	(4m 17.3s)	(1)	4th leg	
25-Apr	Penn Relays	Philadelphia	Distance Medley	(4m 06.5s)	(1)	4th leg	
26-Apr	Penn Relays	Philadelphia	Sprint Medley	...	(1)	4th leg	
26-Apr	Penn Relays	Philadelphia	4 x 440	(48.3s)	(1)	3rd leg	
10-May	Villanova/Army/Syracuse	Villanova	880 Yards	1m 52.1s	(1)		
10-May	Villanova/Army/Syracuse	Villanova	1 Mile	4m 18.3s	(1)		
19-May	Invitational; Santry inaug.	Santry, Dublin	880 Yards	1m 49.9s	(2)	Brian Hewson, 1m 49.7s	
20-May	Invitational; Santry inaug.	Santry, Dublin	1 Mile	4m 07.5s	(1)	Hewson 4m 08.0s	

DATE 1958	MEET	LOCATION	EVENT	TIME	PLACED	NOTES
24-May	vs. La Salle	Villanova	880 Yards	1m 54.9s	(1)	
24-May	vs. La Salle	Villanova	1 Mile	4m 25.2s	(1)	
31-May	IC4A Outdoor	Villanova	880 Yards	1m 50.0s	(1)	Ed Moran
31-May	IC4A Outdoor	Villanova	1 Mile	4m 07.8s	(1)	Ed Moran
06-Jun	Compton Invitational	Compton, Ca.	1 Mile	4m 10.0s	(3)	Herb Elliott, Laszlo Tabori
13-Jun	NCAA Outdoor	Berkeley	880 Yards, ht.	1m 50.2s	(1)	
14-Jun	NCAA Outdoor	Berkeley	1 Mile	4m 03.5s	(1)	Jim Grelle, Gail Hodgson, Don Bowden. RMD splits, 61.4; 63.4; 61.2; 57.5
14-Jun	NCAA Outdoor	Berkeley	880 Yards	1m 48.6s	(1) Tom Murphy. RMD	splits 54.8+28.6+25.2
20-Jun	Clonliffe Invitational	Santry, Dublin	1 Mile	4m 12.5s	(1)	Mick Hoey (4m 12.6s).
02-Jul	Civil Service Invitational	Santry, Dublin	880 Yards	1m 54.0s	(1) Derek McCleane,	Paul Toomey
09-Jul	AAU Invitational	Santry, Dublin	880 Yards	1m 48.5s	(1) Derek McCleane,	Paul Toomey
18-Jul	Invitational	Oslo	1500 Metres	3m 44.8s	(1)	Ulf Bertil Lundh, 3m 45.8s; Arne Hamarsland, 3m 46.0s.
22-Jul	Invitational	Aalberg, Denmark.	1500 Metres	3m 51.3s	(1)	Benny Stender, DEN, 3m 51.4s
06-Aug	**Invitational**	**Santry, Dublin**	**1 Mile**	**3m 57.5s NR**	**(3)**	**Herb Elliott 3:54.5s WR; Merv Lincoln, 3m 55.9s; (Murray Halberg, 3m 57.5s; Albert Thomas, 3m 58.6s).**
07-Aug	Invitational	Santry, Dublin	880 Yards	1m 52.7s	(1)	Donal Smith, NZL; George Kerr; Mal Spence; Merv Lincoln. A great dirty race, with lots of elbows.
22-Aug	European Championships	Stockholm	1500m, ht.2	3m 47.0s	(1)	Olavi Salsola; Ulf Bertil Lundh;
24-Aug	European Championships	Stockholm	1500 Metres	3m 42.3s	(3)	Brian Hewson, Dan Waern

DATE 1959	MEET	LOCATION	EVENT	TIME	PLACED	NOTES	
17-Jan	Mass. Knights of Col.	Boston	1 Mile	4m 08.3s	(1)	Bill Dellinger, Phil Coleman.	30
31-Jan	Millrose Games	Madison Sq. Gdns., NY	1 Mile	4m 06.5s	(1)	Bill Dellinger, Phil Coleman,Zbigniew Orywal	31
07-Feb	Boston AA	Boston	1 Mile	4m 04.3s	(1)	Phil Coleman, Dan Waern, Ed Moran	32
13-Feb	Philadelphia Inquirer	Philadelphia	1 Mile	4m 05.8s	(1)	Laszlo Tabori, Jim Grelle, Coleman, Hewson, Waern	33
14-Feb	NYAC Games	Madison Sq. Gdns., NY	880 Yards	1m 52.2s	(1)	Tom Murphy,Arnie Sowell, Mike Rawson	34
21-Feb	*US AAU Indoor*	*Madison Sq. Gdns., NY*	*1 Mile*	*4m 02.5s WR*	*(1)*	*Istvan Roszavolgyi, Laszlo Tabori, Pete Close*	35
28-Feb	IC4A - Invitational	Madison Sq. Gdns., NY	1 Mile	4m 07.1s	(1)	Phil Coleman, Bill Dellinger,Paul Schmidt	36
07-Mar	*NY Knights of Columbus*	*Madison Sq. Gdns., NY*	*1 Mile*	*4m 01.4s WR*	*(1)*	*Istvan Roszavolgyi*	37
09-Mar	Milwaukee Journal	Milwaukee	1 Mile	4m 05.4s	(1)	Istvan Roszavolgyi, Phil Coleman	38
17-Mar	Optimists Invitational	Hollywood, Fla.	1 Mile	4m 07.8s	(1)	Pete Close, Laszlo Tabori	
20-Mar	Cleveland K. of C.	Cleveland	1 Mile	4m 06.6s	(1)	Istvan Roszavolgyi, Pete Close	39
28-Mar	Chicago Daily News	Chicago	1 Mile	4m 06.4s	(1)	Ed Moran, Phil Coleman. This was 40th consecutive win indoors.	40

DATE 1960	MEET	LOCATION	EVENT	TIME	PLACED	NOTES
31 Aug am	Olympic Games	Rome	800 Metres, Rd. 1	1m 51.0s	(3)	Paul Schmidt, Rudolf Klaban
31 Aug pm	Olympic Games	Rome	800 Metres, Rd. 2	1m 51.1s	(6)	George Kerr, Ernie Cunliffe,Tony Blue
22-Sep	Invitational	Santry, Dublin	880 Yards	1m 48.2s	(2)	Peter Snell... (Tony Blue, Herb Elliott)

DATE 1961	MEET	LOCATION	EVENT	TIME	PLACED	NOTES
05-Jul	AAU v NIAAA	Drogheda	440 Yards	49.4s	(1)	
14-Jul	AAA Championships	White City, London	880 Yards, ht	1m 52.8s	(2)	George Kerr
14-Jul	AAA Championships	White City, London	880 Yards	1m 51.9s	(2)	George Kerr... (Olavi Salsola, Noel Carroll)
17-Jul	Invitational	Santry, Dublin	880 Yards **800 metres**	1m 48.0s **1m 47.1s NR**	(3)	Peter Snell, George Kerr...(Gary Philpott, Carroll)
29-Jul	Invitational	Cardiff	880 Yards	1m 53.1s	(1)	George Kerr
09-Aug	Invitational	Santry, Dublin	4 x 880 Yards	7m 21.8 ER	(1)	Clifford, McCleane, Carroll, Delaney
10-Aug	Invitational	Dublin	1 Mile	4m 04.3s	(1)	Ken Wood 4m 04.9s. Last lap 55.3s.
31-Aug	Universiade	Sofia	800 Metres, sf	1m 50.7s	(1)	
01-Sep	Universiade	Sofia	800 Metres	1m 51.1s	(1)	

DATE 1962	MEET	LOCATION	EVENT	TIME	PLACED	NOTES
02-Feb	Millrose Games	Madison Sq. Gdns., NY	4 x 880y	...	(1)	7m 38.4s; 4th leg
03-Feb	Boston AA	Boston	4 x 880y	(1m 51.4s)	(1)	7m 34.2s; 4th leg
09-Feb	Philadelphia Inquirer	Philadelphia	4 x 880y	...	(1)	7m 44.2s; 4th leg
16-Feb	NYAC Games	Madison Sq. Gdns., NY	4 x 880y	(1m 51.4s)	(2)	7m 37.8s; 4th leg
02-Mar	NY Knights of Columbanus	Madison Sq. Gdns., NY	4 x 880y		(2)	7m 35.4s; 4th leg